**Dawson:** Blond and handsome, he has it all—and doesn't know it. His passion is to be a film director, but somehow real life just won't follow the script.

**Joey:** Slender and dark-haired, she's shared everything a best friend can share with her buddy Dawson—sleepovers, jokes, and the story of her life. But she's not a kid anymore and neither is he.

**Pacey:** He talks big and he's burning to grow up fast. Now someone's in town who could teach him everything he wants to know.

**Jen:** She's sweet and mature and Dawson's crazy about her. But she's running from a big secret back in the city. Maybe this new girl in town is too much for Dawson to handle.

# DAWSON'S CREEK™

Don't miss any of these
DAWSON'S CREEK™ books!
Long Hot Summer
Major Meltdown
Shifting Into Overdrive
Double Exposure

Read more about
Joey, Dawson, Pacey, and Jen
in four new, original
DAWSON'S CREEK™ stories.
Coming soon from Channel 4 Books.

Check your bookstore to see if they're in yet.

# Dawson's Creek™
## The Beginning of Everything Else

Based on the television series Dawson's Creek
created by and episodes
"Dawson's Creek" and Episode #101
written by Kevin Williamson

Novelization by Jennifer Baker

CHANNEL 4 BOOKS

First published 1998 by Pocket Books, a division of
Simon and Schuster Inc., New York

First published in Great Britain 1999 by Channel 4 Books
an imprint of Macmillan Publishers Ltd
25 Eccleston Place, London SW1W 9NF
Basingstoke and Oxford

Associated companies throughout the world

ISBN 0 7522 1344 X

5 7 9 8 6 4

A CIP catalogue record for this book is available from
the British Library.

Printed and bound in Great Britain by
Mackays of Chatham plc, Chatham, Kent

The Beginning of Everything Else

*Chapter 1*

Outside the window of the big rambling white house, the water shimmered silver in the hazy moonlight. Inside, the TV cast its own glow in Dawson Leery's bedroom.

"I'll be ri-ight he-ere," E.T. promised on the large television screen.

Joey Potter stared at the TV, stretched out on her stomach on the big bed next to Dawson amid the sea of pillows and half-empty bags of Doritos and Oreo Double Stufs.

"I love this movie," Joey gushed. "This won the Oscar, didn't it?" She'd watched it a bunch of times, but she still hated to see it end.

"*Gandhi* won," Dawson corrected her. "Spielberg was robbed," he added with absolute conviction. "This was before he outgrew his Peter Pan syndrome." As the credits rolled, Dawson leveled the remote at the screen and hit the rewind. The local news anchors appeared on the screen, a his-and-hers set of pearly whites and lots of perfectly coiffed hair.

"But *Gandhi*?" Joey said. "Why give an Oscar to a movie you can't even sit through?" She didn't wait for Dawson to answer. She knew he agreed with her. "New do?" she asked, checking out the anchorwoman. It was weird, seeing *her* on TV every night. After all these years, Joey still hadn't quite gotten over it.

"Yeah. She likes big hair," Dawson said.

Joey turned her gaze away from the TV and foraged for her sneakers. The woman wore a Colgate smile. "Back to you, Bob," she told her co-anchor.

"Her hair must weigh a lot." Joey located one sneaker. Then the other. "How does she walk upright?"

Dawson laughed. Joey stuffed her feet into the sneakers and stood up.

"Where ya going?" Dawson asked.

"Home."

"Spend the night," Dawson said matter-of-factly.

"Can't," Joey answered, hoping she sounded just as matter-of-fact. She turned her face away from Dawson, not quite able to look at him.

"You always spend the night." Dawson's words had an edge of surprise.

"Not tonight."

"Why not?"

Joey moved toward the open window. She could

feel the warm late-summer breeze that toyed with the parted blue-and-gray curtains. Didn't Dawson get it? Didn't he see?

She whirled back around to face him—his strong face, his thick, wavy blond hair, his full mouth and deep-set, intelligent hazel eyes—intelligent about movies and stories and drama, at least. But this was *real* life. Dawson had always been able to read her like a script. And she him. So why did she have to spell this one out for him?

"I just don't think it's a good idea for me to sleep over anymore, you know?"

Dawson's solid, square jaw tightened. "No, I don't know! You've been sleeping over since we were seven. It's Saturday night, come on!"

"Things change, Dawson—evolve." Joey stressed this last word, hoping to make her point. "Go with it."

"What are you talking about?"

He was hopeless.

"Sleeping in the same bed was fine when we were kids," Joey began. "But we're fifteen now."

Dawson arched an eyebrow. "Yeah."

"We start high school on Monday."

"Yeah . . ."

Okay, she was going to have to cut to the chase. There just wasn't any other choice. "And I have breasts."

Joey's words hung in the humid air for a second. "What?" Dawson gave a startled laugh.

"And you have genitalia," Joey went on.

3

"I've always had genitalia." Dawson didn't miss a beat this time.

"But there's more of it now," Joey insisted.

She saw Dawson swallow. Okay. Maybe he was hearing her now.

"How do you know?" he asked.

In too deep. It was time for this little conversation to end. "Long fingers," Joey tossed out as she grabbed the window frame and slid one leg out the window. If Dawson didn't get it, she did. And it was time for her to leave.

"Whoa, Joe. Don't hit and run. Explain yourself," Dawson insisted.

Did she have to hit him over the head? Joey reeled herself back inside but stayed near the window. "I just think our emerging hormones are destined to alter our relationship and I'm trying to limit the fallout."

Joey watched her message finally get through. Dawson's eyes opened just a little. He pressed his lips together, but he recovered fast. "Your 'emerging hormones' aren't starting to get a thang for me, are they?"

Well, no. Couldn't be. It was just that she lived in the real world—unlike some people. And she could admit it—she noticed the cut of his jaw in a way she never had before. Noticed his . . . well, his long fingers. Noticed that she noticed. Even though this was Dawson. Same old same old from time immemorial. Or at least from second grade.

"A 'thang'?" Joey volleyed back. "Oh, so typical. No, I'm not getting a thang for you, Dawson. I've known you too long. I've seen you burp, barf, pick your nose, scratch your butt. I'm not getting a thang for you."

"Then what's the problem?"

Joey felt an electric trill of annoyance. "We're changing, and we have to adjust or the male-female thing will get in the way."

Dawson's irritation mirrored hers. "What is with the When Harry Met the Eighties crap? It doesn't apply to us. We transcend it."

"And how do we do that?"

"By going to sleep. I'm tired," Dawson said.

Right. Close your eyes to it, and it will go away. "That's avoidance," Joey told him, turning back to the window.

"No, it's proof. Proof that we can still remain friends despite any mounting sexual theoretics," Dawson said.

Go to sleep. Lie down together and go right to sleep. Nothing more. In the same bed, but separate. Proof. Well, maybe that *was* one way of showing they were friends and friends only. Maybe Dawson actually had a point there. Or maybe Joey just didn't really want to go home all that awfully. Things were better at Dawson's house than at hers. Better with Dawson. Had been ever since . . .

"I don't think it works that way Dawson," Joey said uncertainly. She felt the breeze blowing off the creek and through the window.

Dawson did an exaggerated back-flop onto his bed. "C'mon, don't get female on me, Joey. I don't wanna have to start calling you Josephine."

The sound of that name on Dawson's lips—it went straight to Joey's gut. Do not process through the brain. Do not pass go. "Josephine this," she said, taking a flying dive at Dawson. She landed smack on top of him and slugged him in the shoulder.

"Hey!" He seized her arms, his hands circling her slender forearms.

Joey shook them off.

Dawson moved in again, grabbing her in a bear hug and rolling her underneath him.

Joey struggled, her laugh slightly breathless. Dawson had her pinned down. His face was inches away from hers. Joey stopped struggling and looked up at him. "Okay, I give." Dawson grew suddenly still as well.

He flopped back down next to her. "We're friends, okay? No matter how much body hair we acquire. Deal?"

"Deal," Joey agreed. Of course they were friends. This was Dawson. She pushed her sneakers off and heard them fall to the floor with a soft thud.

"And we don't talk about this again, deal?" Dawson said.

"You got it," Joey said, staring up at the white ceiling. She certainly didn't want to do this one over again.

"Cool," Dawson said.

"Cool," Joey echoed with a note of uncertainty. She turned onto her side, away from Dawson, but she wasn't comfortable. She curled up, then stretched out again. Dawson was also squirming around next to her. She felt him moving around, pulling at the sheet.

"Good night, Joey," he said. He hit the light switch. The room went shadowy, but the moonlight filtering in through the curtains seemed to grow brighter.

"Night, Dawson," Joey answered.

She still couldn't get comfortable, but she willed herself to lie still. As her body finally started to relax, Dawson broke the silence.

"Why did you have to bring this up, anyway?" he asked.

# Chapter 2

Joey was stretched out on the dock in a deck chair, her long, slim, gently bronzed body in white shorts, a light shirt open over her plaid bikini top, her long, dark hair loose in the breeze. The last sun of summer warmed her bare skin. The air smelled of salt water and the warm wood of the dock at the edge of the creek. A couple of guys raced by on Sunfishes, their sails bright against the blue sky.

It was a picture-perfect afternoon. A picture-perfect setting. One of the loveliest parts of a lovely town—a salty inlet winding in from the ocean and widening at this point into a gentle lagoon complete with sea grasses and a gray heron spreading its majestic wings and rising up off the water.

Joey was lying near Dawson's oversize but unpretentious house, but her eyes were closed to it as she took in the sun.

Suddenly the dock shook. Joey's eyes flew open as a slimy slate-green mega-huge sea monster split the surface of the water and rose up to grab her!

She let out a terrified scream. It was trying to pull her into the water! She struggled, straining every muscle in her body. She tucked her arm in close to her side and then let rip with a sharp elbow to the creature's belly.

The sea creature let out a yelp and sank back into the muddy depths but managed to take Joey along, chair and all.

"No! No! Cut!" Dawson yelled, pulling back from the camera mounted on its tripod. "Cut! Wait a second. You gotta wait three counts for that."

Out in the water, Joey shot a furious look at the sea creature as it pulled itself up onto the dock. She pushed him away and got out before he did.

"If you attack her before the scene is established, it's not scary," Dawson yelled. Now he'd never get that shot.

"He did it again. He grabbed my ass!" Joey yelled.

"Like you even have one," the sea creature shot back. He peeled his mask off—the mask Dawson had spent all week working on. Pacey's face appeared—his mouth open, as slack and gangly as the rest of him, his short, dark brown hair wet.

Dawson took a few quick steps toward them. "Guys, guys, you're killing me. We're way behind schedule. I'm never going to make the festival. I've got two months." These were supposed to be his best friends. "Hel-*lo!* Cooperation!"

"I'm not playing the victim," Joey mumbled.

Pacey pointed a green-gray rubber claw at her. "It's Meryl Streep's fault," he said, nonplussed. "I'm doing the best I can."

Joey spat out her annoyance. "Bite me!" she told Pacey disgustedly.

Dawson heard a car pulling up behind him, tires on the gravel driveway of his neighbors' house. He glanced over his shoulder as a yellow cab pulled to a stop.

He turned back to his camera for a moment, took a fresh video cartridge from the camera bag at his feet, and began to reload. His fingers worked as quickly as possible.

"Guys, from the top," he said, firmly. "And make me believe it. I want the truth."

He shot them a stern look, but Pacey was staring right past him. "Well, well . . . my mouth drops," Pacey said.

Dawson looked back at the taxi, then turned his whole body. A girl had stepped out. Her short, cream-colored sundress revealed her great curves. A light sea breeze blew her shoulder-length, honey-blond hair away from her delicate round face, and Dawson could see that she was way pretty. Beautiful. He felt his breath catch.

She smiled at them and came right over—no timid ready-to-fade flower, either. She made her way down the dock. A locket on a dainty gold chain around her neck winked in the sun.

Dawson took a quick look back at Pacey and Joey. Pacey was staring at the beautiful girl, as dumbstruck as—a sea creature. But Joey was looking right at Dawson. He arched an eyebrow at her and turned back toward the girl.

"Hey, you guys!" The girl's greeting was open and friendly.

Pacey jumped right in without a breath. "How's it going? I'm Pacey." He grabbed her hand and shook it.

Dawson followed. "I'm—"

"Dawson. I know. We've met before," the girl said. They shook, too. Her hand was warm. "I'm Jen."

Jen. The house next door. Whoa! "Okay, you're the granddaughter from New York," Dawson said. "You look so . . . different." Reluctantly he released her hand.

Dawson felt Joey step up beside him. "Puberty," she deadpanned. Dawson didn't know if he was supposed to feel embarrassed. "Hi, I'm Joey," she continued. "I live down the creek, and we've never met. Ever." Whatever.

"So are you just visiting?" Dawson asked Jen. He noticed the cabdriver unloading a couple of large suitcases. They looked as if they could hold a lot of sundresses.

"My grandfather's aorta collapsed, and they had to replace it with a plastic tube," Jen recited. "My parents sent me to help out for a while."

Yeah, Dawson had heard about the old guy next

door. Pretty serious stuff. So Jen might be around for some time. "So you'll be going to school here?"

"Yeah," Jen confirmed. "Tenth grade." She had a nice easygoing smile.

"Cool!" Pacey jumped in, overeager. "Us, too."

Jen nodded. A flock of seagulls passed overhead, screaming noisily as they wheeled and darted. "Well . . . Grams must be waiting," Jen said. "I should go. It was nice to meet you, guys. See ya at school."

"If not sooner," Dawson heard himself saying.

Jen smiled again. At him. Her eyes stayed on him for an extra beat. Dawson felt a wave of pleasurable embarrassment. Man, the girl was cute. She turned around and headed for the gate in the neat low fence that separated her grandparents' yard from Dawson's.

He watched her move toward the porch of the elegant white house with the blue trim. She looked back once and gave a last little wave before going inside.

Dawson continued to stare at the deserted porch.

"If not sooner," he heard Joey mimic before she brushed past him and took off in the other direction.

"Nice," Pacey commented, also still staring at the house next door.

"All right," Dawson agreed.

Pacey draped the wet monster suit over the slender wood railing of Dawson's back porch. It glistened in the sun like the wet suit of some demented diver.

Well, thought Dawson distractedly, Pacey can be pretty demented, sometimes. We got that much right. His mind was half on a bunch of things—his movie, Joey's weirdness lately—but at the same time it was totally on one thing: his new neighbor.

"Think she's a virgin?" Pacey asked. "You gonna nail her?"

Dawson was used to Pacey's bluntness. Its shock value was lost on him. He let himself in through the screen door and stashed his camera equipment in a corner of the mudroom. "We just met," he told Pacey evenly as his friend followed him inside.

"And a wasted moment it was." Pacey didn't let up. "Greater men would be nailing right now."

"Tact," Dawson said. "Look it up."

Before Pacey could parry, an impressive crash sounded from deep inside the house—some heavy object meeting its death as it struck a hard floor. Dawson and Pacey exchanged a quick glance and took off in the direction of the noise. Through the green-walled foyer, down the hall, and into the open, sun-drenched heart of the house. At the far end, the all-new kitchen gleamed in stainless steel and bright tile. The spacious living area rose two stories to the dark rough-hewn rafters that crossed the solid plaster-white ceiling at intervals. Another staircase led from a corner up to the second-floor landing that overlooked the room.

In front of the brick fireplace a man and a woman

were pressed together atop the coffee table, kissing passionately. Dawson froze, Pacey by his side.

"Oh, no," Dawson moaned. "Mom . . ." he protested.

His parents pulled apart quickly and looked up at him, and his mother rolled off the table and onto the floor. Busted!

Between her and the big-screen TV, a Mexican water jug lay broken, shards of terra-cotta littering the smoothly finished wide-plank floors.

Next to him, Dawson knew Pacey was staring, agape. Dawson could feel himself turning three shades of cooked lobster.

"Oh, hi, son," his father said sheepishly.

"Whoops," his mother said, sitting up and looking at him. The face of the local news, Mrs. Leery—otherwise known as dear old mom. She straightened her blouse and made a pass at patting her hair into place—the new do Joey had noticed the other night on TV.

"Your mom and I," said his father, "were . . ."

". . . just discussing whether or not . . ." his mother continued, groping to ad lib.

". . . we needed a new coffee table," Mr. Leery finished, as if he might even believe it.

Mrs. Leery gave an embarrassed laugh.

Mr. Leery stood up. "Hi, Pacey."

"Hi, Mr. Leery. Mrs. Leery," Pacey said brightly. Dawson sneaked a look at him. He was grinning from ear to ear, loving every minute of Dawson's shame. Toast. That's what he was if he said a word about this later.

"Hi, Pacey," Dawson's mother said from the floor. "Don't look so red, Dawson. It could be worse."

Right. Good morning to you, too, Mom. At least their clothes were still on. Maybe that was what his mom meant.

"I really love your new hairdo, Mrs. Leery," said Pacey.

"Oh, thank you, Pacey." Mom was recovering fast. And Pacey—the guy couldn't stop staring. And smirking.

"I thought you guys had to work today," Dawson's dad said.

"We're running late," Dawson replied. As if he was the one who needed to explain.

"Me too," his mother said. "I should get going." She stood up and straightened her skirt. Then she glanced over at Dawson's father. She gave him a private smile. "Okay, Mr. Man Meat, I'll see you later." She bent down and gave him a kiss. Really getting into it.

Dawson was aghast. He wished he could blast the swamp-licking grin right off Pacey's face.

"Oh, Mom . . ."

Joey pulled twice on one oar, then straightened out a little with a light pull on the other. She expertly steered the little rowboat up the creek toward her dock. You couldn't help noticing the difference between her house and Dawson's. At least she couldn't, even though she didn't want to.

It wasn't so much that her house was smaller—

though it was, a little. And the view of the creek here in the marshes was just as pretty, all blue-green water and waving grasses and the coveted privacy of a spot with not a single other house in sight. But the gray shingles of the low ranch-style house were worn, and the paint was peeling off the trim. You could see that the roof needed work, too. True, Bess and Bodie had brightened up the yard with lots of plants and flowers and homemade touches, but the place needed some professional care.

Joey tried to ignore the way the house looked as she hopped out of the boat and tied it to the dock. She made her way toward the wide front porch just as the door flew open.

Out stepped a tall, fit black man, in his early twenties. Handsome, an open smile on his face. He had on a crisp white T-shirt and carried a heavy cooking pot carefully in one hand, a wooden spoon in the other. "Just the victim I'm looking for," he said, coming toward Joey with the spoon pointed at her.

"No, Bodie!" Joey put a hand up. "Not again."

"I'm being tested on this one," he pleaded. "Just a taste."

Actually, it smelled good. Some garlic-rich, tomatoey potion. Joey obliged him. It was delicious. A smooth, velvety puree with bits of some pillowy pastalike thing that melted in her mouth.

"Orgasmic," she said. "Where's Bess?"

"Right here." Her sister's voice preceded her. Bess moved out onto the porch with slow steps, a hand on the small of her back, her belly hugely swollen with pregnancy. Somehow she still managed to come off looking good in her simple but elegant long dress, and necklace of tiny freshwater pearl beads. Ever the beautiful older sister.

The look on her face, however, was another story. And in her hand was a rumpled blue T-shirt—the one Joey had borrowed out of her sister's drawer the other day. Oops.

"If you want to wear my things, fine," Bess said harshly. "They're fairly useless to me at this point. But that means you put them back where you found them. Got it?"

"Got it," Joey said flatly. Okay, she knew Bess was tired. Scared, probably. You could see it in her eyes, and it made the seven-year difference between them seem bigger than ever. But Bess had no excuse for taking everything out on Joey. This had to be the longest pregnancy on human record.

"I am way too pregnant to be digging underneath your bed," Bess chastised.

"So stay out of my room," Joey shot back. "Got it?" She pushed past her sister and headed toward the door.

"I'm gonna knock her silly, I swear it," she heard Bess tell Bodie. She turned to shoot her sister a look. But Bodie was approaching Bess with the spoon now.

"Here, try this," he said easily, soothingly.

As Bess bent down to take a taste, Bodie leaned in and lingeringly kissed the curve of her neck.

"Orgasmic," Joey thought she heard her sister say.

*Chapter 3*

It was starting to quiet down in town. Finally. Some leftover tourists were still browsing in the shops, purchasing T-shirts with oysters printed on them and toy plastic sharks at an end-of-season discount, but there was a little more breathing room, and more of the faces were familiar. The S.S. Icehouse wasn't quite empty, but the waitresses were taking it easy, finding smiles that had been buried in the sand all through August. For a town whose unspoiled, undiscovered charm was its draw, an awful lot of people managed to discover it during the summer months. Now the postcard-pretty town of Capeside belonged to the Capesiders again.

Inside the video store Pacey stood behind the counter logging in the returns—all the big summer hits. Next to him, in a matching blue Screenplay

Video vest, Dawson was doing the same. A customer wandered around the new releases.

"Hey." Pacey couldn't resist razzing Dawson. "If your dad is Mr. Man Meat, does that make you Man Meat Junior or Man Meat the Second?" That scene in Dawson's living room had been great, Pacey gloated. Just great. Dawson couldn't have done it any better in one of his movies.

"They're gonna have to drag the creek to find your body," Dawson threatened.

Suddenly Nellie appeared in the comedy aisle, waving a video. Bad timing. Pacey was just getting started on Dawson. Of course, Nellie was always bad timing, no matter what was going down. A self-styled starlet with unnaturally blond ringlets and lips as red as a stop sign, Nellie was a nightmare caricature of Courtney Love meets Marilyn Monroe meets Shirley Temple with a little Cyndi Lauper dredged up from the eighties, just in case. Pacey was glad the vests looked better on him and Dawson.

"Does *Forrest Gump* go in the comedy or drama section?" she asked.

"How many times you gonna ask that?" Pacey answered her question with a question.

"It goes in the drama section," Dawson supplied the answer.

"Thank you, Dawson," Nellie said pointedly, looking hard at Pacey. Then she whirled and headed for drama.

"Can you say wet brain?" Pacey mumbled under his breath.

Nellie whirled back, her face livid. "I'm sorry,"

she said, her tone distinctly belying her words. "What did you say? Did you toss a disparaging remark my way? Because if you did, and correct me if I'm wrong, I'd like to remind you who you are."

Pacey gave an unruffled shrug. "I know. I know. Your dad owns this store."

"No, I'm talking about in the huge rotating world of life," Nellie spat out dramatically, as heated as Pacey was placid.

"And who am I, Nellie?" he asked, not caring much what she answered.

"Nobody. That's the point. You're not there. You don't even exist. 'Cause if you did, I might have to respond to your pathetic little under-your-breath one-liners, but instead I take comfort knowing you're vapor. *Pphhhhtt!*" Nellie did her mist-out-of-a-spray-can imitation. "*Pphhhhtt!*" She waved her hands around in front of her to signal that Pacey had disappeared into thin air. "Nonexistent nothing. *Pphhhhtt!*" She was clearly pleased with the way she was playing this scene.

Oooh. Pacey watched her walk off. Wet brain.

The jingle of bells over the door announced the arrival of another customer. Pacey looked toward the door and felt his face flush. The woman was gorgeous, wearing a short dress, her dark blond hair curving just past her shoulders, high cheekbones—the whole nine yards. Okay, she wasn't exactly Pacey's age. But she was curvy in all the right places, and she walked it, and her face was still at least a 9. Or a 9.5.

"Oh, my God. Look at her," Pacey said softly.

Dawson looked up, too. "Show some respect," he said. "She's somebody's mother."

Yes, Dawson had just set himself up. "I have it on good authority that mothers have great sex lives," Pacey said, waggling his eyebrows.

The woman moved toward the counter. She smiled. At Pacey. He went warm.

"Good afternoon," Pacey heard Dawson say. "Can we help you?"

"Yes, you can," she said, her voice smooth. "This is my first time here, and I'd like to rent a video."

Pacey grabbed a Screenplay Video membership application and stepped in front of Dawson. "Excellent. Just fill this out and shoot me a credit card." He edged Dawson out of the way.

Dawson obliged, grabbing a stack of videos and heading for the shelves. The woman started filling out the card, long, slender fingers holding the pen.

"So are you new in town?" Pacey asked. "I haven't seen you around." The good ones were always from somewhere else.

She looked right into his eyes. Hazel eyes, long lashes. A few delicate lines around the eyes, but they were sexy. Experienced. "Yes, I am. My name's Tamara." There was a sexy lilt to her words. "What's yours?"

"Pacey." He gulped. "Nice to meet you."

Tamara slid the application back across the counter along with her credit card. She continued to hold Pacey's gaze.

He looked right back at her. Couldn't look away. "Can I help you locate a video this afternoon?"

21

"Maybe. I'm in the mood for romance." He'd heard it. Straight from her luscious lips. She smiled at him.

He was hers. Her slave. "Uh . . . well, the new releases are—"

"No," Tamara interjected. "I'm vintage. All the way," she added.

Right on that one. The woman was severely hot. Pacey could barely move his mouth. "Uh . . . uh . . . the classics are—"

"Where would I find *The Graduate*?" she asked.

He wasn't imagining this. "*The Graduate*? Let's see . . . that was the one—"

"Where older woman Anne Bancroft seduces younger man Dustin Hoffman."

Pacey swallowed, his throat dry. "Uh, let me check."

Dawson appeared like a meddlesome big brother, video in hand. He held it out to Tamara. "It's right here, actually. Anything else we can help you with this afternoon?" he asked easily.

Back in the bottle, Dawson.

"No. That should do it," Tamara said. "How much?"

Too late. Dawson had spoiled the party.

"Pay when you return," Dawson said. "Don't forget your credit card." He slid it back toward her. "Enjoy the film."

"I will," Tamara said. She turned to leave. But she looked back over her shoulder and gave Pacey one more slow smile. "It was nice to meet you, Pacey."

"Uh, yeah . . . uh-huh," Pacey agreed, unable to find his tongue. He watched her walk toward the door—the gentle roll of her hips, the curve of her calves. The bells jingled as she left the store.

"Wipe the drool, dude," Dawson said.

"She was flirting with me," Pacey marveled.

"She was laughing at you."

"No way." Pacey was sure. He'd felt it. He'd heard the way she talked, felt her eyes holding him. "She wanted me," he said, feeling an expansion of his ego.

"She wanted Dustin Hoffman." Dawson took another stack of videos and went back to shelving them with Nellie. Pacey stared at the door, his last glimpse of Tamara burned into his mind.

Dawson appeared from around the corner of his house, balancing a pile of videos under one arm. The sun was low, swollen, and red over the far end of the creek and the gently rolling landscape. The sky around the sun was shot with pink and yellow, the bellies of the wispy clouds reflecting the fiery colors in a deepening blue sky overhead. Out toward the ocean, a sliver of moon had already risen.

Dawson saw her right away. Felt her even before he saw her. Jen was sitting on the dock, her feet dangling in the water. She was silhouetted against the setting sun. Perfect profile. He hesitated. Should he go over? She looked pretty peaceful. He took an uncertain step toward her, then stopped.

She turned toward him. Spotted him. "Hey!" she gave a little wave.

Dawson felt a breeze of relief. "Hey." He felt a little out of breath. "How's your granddad?" He sat down next to her. Close. But not too.

"Well . . . he's breathing—good sign," Jen said with a tentative laugh. "Grams, however, presents a challenge. She has this praying mentality. Always saying grace, which is really uncomfortable, since I don't do the God thing."

Jen glanced at the stack of videos Dawson was holding.

"Let's see what you've got here." Jen reached for his videotapes, moving on to an easier subject. "*Swamp Thing. Humanoids from the Deep? Creature from the Black Lagoon?*"

"Research," he told her. "I'm making a movie."

"You're really young to be so ambitious." Jen sounded impressed.

Dawson felt a shudder of pride. But he didn't want to come on too puffed up. "I'm fifteen. Spielberg started on eight millimeter when he was thirteen."

"And why the movies?" Jen asked. "What's the attraction there?"

Easy one. He'd been over this footage before. "I reject reality."

"Oh!" Jen laughed.

"Would you like to see my studio?" Dawson asked, taking a chance.

Jen smiled right away.

\*　　\*　　\*

Dawson's room was a shrine to Steven Spielberg. Posters lined every wall; a stuffed E.T. doll sat on a shelf next to a miniature great white shark, the famous jaws tamed in hard plastic. Toy dinosaurs, big and small—Jurassic era only—stalked across the floor. A framed photo of the man himself occupied a place of honor on Dawson's desk.

Dawson watched Jen take it all in. "Long shot. Spielberg fan?" she noted.

"I pretty much worship the man," Dawson admitted.

"Revealing," Jen said. Did that mean good or bad?

"I've chronicled his career on these walls," Dawson said, making fun of himself a little. "You'll notice everything is arranged in receding box-office order, starting with the blockbusters. *Jurassic Park*, *E.T.*, *Jaws*, the Indiana Jones series." He pointed around the room. "And you follow them around to the critically acclaimed wall." Jen eyed the posters that lined the walls of Dawson's room.

"Are you familiar with obsessive reality disorders?" Jen joked.

"It's beyond that," Dawson said, playing at a touch of vanity. "I firmly believe that the mysteries of the universe, the answers to all of life's questions, can be found in a Spielberg film. It's a theory I've been working on. Whenever I have a problem, all I have to do is look to the right Spielberg movie and the answer is revealed."

Jen arched a blond eyebrow. "Have you considered a twelve-step program?"

"Wit. We like that around here," Dawson said. Man, she thought as sharp as she looked.

"So that was your own movie you were shooting this morning, out on the dock?"

"Yeah. The Boston film critics offer this program for junior filmmakers. Heavy competition. The deadline's in two months. I'm really under the gun."

"Jennifer!" He heard a woman's voice outside calling. It was far away, but he didn't miss the edge.

Jen went over to the window. Dawson moved next to her and looked out. He could see the shadowy outline of the lady next door, standing on her porch. Jen's grandmother.

"I'd better go," Jen said. I don't want her to erupt." She took a few steps toward the door. "Later."

"See ya at school," Dawson said. As Jen raced out, he let the smile stretch across his face. He turned to the Spielberg photo. "Nice, huh?"

Joey got a sour taste in her mouth. She balanced precariously at the top of the ladder up to the second floor of Dawson's home.

She watched Jen run across the grass toward her grandparents' house. The new girl worked fast. First day here and she'd already had the tour of Dawson's bedroom.

Joey climbed onto the porch roof and looked through Dawson's window. She saw him grab two remotes. He clicked one of them and the TV popped on. He clicked the other and the VCR did its stuff.

A tape of his mother's news show came into focus. What was he doing?

Joey climbed in through the window.

Dawson looked up. "Hey, Joe, where have you been? Watch this."

As Joey settled down in front of the television, Dawson hit the Rewind button, then Play. His mother appeared, big hair, dishing out the news. "Call 555-5982," she announced. The camera pulled back to reveal her co-anchor next to her. "Back to you, Bob."

"Do you think my mom's sleeping with him?" Dawson asked.

Joey stared at Dawson. "Where did that come from?" Dawson had succeeded in distracting her from thoughts of that Jen person. At least a little.

"Watch," Dawson instructed. He rewound a few seconds of the tape, then pressed Play again.

On the TV screen, his mother looked over at her co-anchor. "Back to you, Bob," she said again, just as she always did.

"Something about her *b*'s," Dawson insisted. "They're too soft. 'Bbback to you, Bbbobb.' See?" He worked the remote and played it again.

"You're reaching," Joey said. "Why would your mom be sleeping with her co-anchor? Your dad's the perfect male specimen." Dawson looked kind of like him, actually.

"I don't know, but I think they are," Dawson said.

"You're just looking for conflict. Everything's a potential script to you. Accept your perfect life,

Dawson. It's a reality." Everyone should have it so good. Joey felt more annoyed than usual by Dawson's attitude. He had everything. Everything.

Joey glanced out the window, letting out a breath. Across the way, she could see Jen stepping onto her porch. The new girl. The bright, sunny new girl. And now it looked as if Dawson wanted her in addition to everything else. Joey turned back to Dawson. Passing on a reply to her outburst, he continued to watch his mother broadcasting the news.

Joey watched him watch. The face she knew so well. They'd agreed they were friends. Always friends. They wanted it that way. Joey had been his number one pal forever. The one he hung with. The one he told stuff to. Even if they were just being friends. Especially because they were just about being friends. Dawson insisted that didn't have to change. Ever. But Dawson didn't do reality that well. He'd never had to.

# Chapter 4

The sun was hot already. It was still low in the morning sky, but it glinted powerfully off the creek. Jen could see it out her window—the window of her new bedroom in her grandparents' house. Not exactly the steel and brick and glass towers she was used to seeing when she got out of bed. Jen could feel the humid warmth rising off the water and filling her room as she dressed for the first day of her new school.

Short white denim skirt, pale blue short-sleeved cardigan. She glanced in the mirror over her dresser. Lower key than she would have chosen back in New York. Fine. It wasn't a fashion show around these parts. That was for sure. And just as well, probably. She grabbed her big canvas bag, a new notebook inside, and slung it over her shoulder.

She stepped out of her room and started down the hall.

Her grandfather's door was partly open. She stopped. She peered in, nudging it open farther with her arm. She could see her grandfather sleeping in his big bed in the center of the room. There wasn't a whole lot else in there. A chair. A bureau. A nightstand—with a pharmacopoeia of prescription bottles on top of it. Drugs. Jen felt a tremor of worry.

Quietly she entered the room. She got up close to her grandfather and watched him sleep. He looked pretty good, considering . . .

"G'morning, Grindeddy," she said gently.

One arm was outside the covers, his hand as fragile as a little bird, the skin papery thin and translucent, the delicate network of blood vessels clearly visible. His life was flowing through those veins and arteries. Jen reached out hesitantly. She let one finger touch his hand, lightly tracing a line of purplish blue. His hand felt more solid than it looked. She glanced at his face, but there was no reaction to her touch.

She took his whole hand in hers. Squeezed gently but firmly. Still nothing. Her eyes moved to his chest, rising and falling almost imperceptibly. His pajama shirt was open at the top. She focused on the bare, hairless skin. She felt a wave of curiosity. And tenderness. They'd opened him up like a cleaved chicken. Seen inside him. Held his heart in their hands. His life in their hands.

She let go of his hand and parted his pajama top

farther. She sucked in her breath sharply. A huge dark scar appeared. The massive cut had been stitched meticulously, and shiny new skin had grown over it, but it was still gruesomely impressive.

"What are you doing?"

Jen's pulse skipped a beat. She spun around to face her grandmother. "Uh . . . I was just . . . saying good morning."

Grams had a faintly distrusting shine in her pale eyes. "Your breakfast is ready," she said rather stiffly.

Grams looked younger than most of Jen's friends' grandparents, or at least she would have without that old-lady apron over her prim skirt and blouse, her hair pulled back severely, brown shot with gray. But the reserved, slightly starched way she held herself made her seem far older.

She and Jen looked at each other guardedly. What did Grams think? She'd just been spending time with her grandfather. Jen felt the silence between them. How had she let herself wind up here? Then she glanced at her grandfather, sleeping, and she felt the tension drain out of her.

"I'm glad I'm here, Grams." And as she said it, she knew she meant it. This was Grams, whom she'd spent summers with as a little girl. Grams and Gramps, whom she loved. It was going to be better here. Jen was going to make sure of that.

Grams kept Jen in check with her gaze for another moment. Then she seemed to give in a little. "You'd better hurry. You don't want to be late your first day."

First day. New school. Jen felt a trill of nerves. She wasn't exactly dying to get there, except maybe to get it over with.

A few minutes later she was seated at the heavy oak table in her grandmother's big old kitchen. Small pots of herbs grew on the sunny windowsill. Grams bustled around at the vintage stove, adjusting the flame on the gas burners and stirring and flipping the contents of two black cast-iron skillets. The smell of bacon and coffee filled the air.

"You know, I usually don't eat in the morning," Jen informed her grandmother as she set a huge plate of bacon and eggs in front of her. "I appreciate the fuss, though." She didn't want Grams to frost over again. "But my eyes don't even open till noon. A coffee fix and I'm set."

Grams poured a mug of java. "I'll remember that in the future," she said, not betraying any emotion. She put a cup of coffee down at Jen's place and poured herself a cup, too.

Jen took a sip. Strong. Black. Good. That much Grams had down. "So tell me about this Dawson-guy next door. He looks so different. He used to be short and compact." She thought about how Dawson looked now. And allowed herself a smile.

She felt Grams eyeing her. "You stay away. The boy's trouble."

"Aren't they all," Jen said more lightly than she felt. "And that girl from down the creek—Joey, I think her name is?"

Grams definitely did not like the way this was going. "That girl from down the creek has been crawling into the bedroom window of that boy next door for the past ten years."

Yeah? Jen felt a pinch of surprise. And disappointment. She didn't think she'd read Dawson wrong.

"And neither one of them goes to church," Grams added. "I believe they're what you call the wrong element."

Wrong. "Right," Jen said.

Her grandmother carried her own plate of breakfast to the table. She sat down next to Jen and pressed her hands together in prayer. "Say grace, dear."

Jen looked into her coffee mug. "That's okay. You can say it," she said quietly.

"It would be nice if you would say grace."

Now what? "I don't think so, Grams. Thanks, though," Jen said politely.

Her grandmother's face grew tight. "Is there some reason you don't want to thank our Lord this morning?"

Jen passed her hand through her hair. She was trying, but Grams was pushing it. "Oh, Grams, I didn't really want to get into this, since I just got here and I'm kind of prone to headaches," she threw in, "but I don't do well with prayer and church and that Bible stuff."

The fragile truce with Grams was over. "I beg your pardon?"

There was only one way to tell it—straight out. "I don't believe in a religious god. I'm an atheist," Jen said as honestly and gently as she could. There.

33

She'd told it. Her grandmother stared at her, too shocked to muster up a response. Her praying hands dropped to the table.

Dawson lay in bed, half watching the morning news. "A maritime disaster leaves forty-three dead in India," the newscaster announced. "And we'll have a bright, sunny day today. More when we get back."

Outside, a door slammed. The door of the house across the way. Dawson sat right up in bed, looking out his window. Jen! All long, shapely arms and legs in a sky-blue top and a short white skirt, her hair shining in the daylight. She headed down her grandparents' walkway, a vision of high school loveliness toting a book bag.

Dawson was out of bed. His bare feet hit the floor. This boy had places to go.

It looked like a school. Any school. Every school. The perfect school. The perfect small-town school, set back on a green lawn, a three-story red-brown brick building with wide steps leading up to the main doors, a clock with Roman numerals above the entrance, showing another quarter of an hour before anyone really had to be anywhere. Kids all over the place, heading into the building, spilling over the lawn, trading high fives, low fives, news of the summer. Music poured out across the grass, a rap rhythm blasting from someone's boom box. Two guys passed a football. A girl with long red hair

34

tossed a Frisbee to her friend. A couple kissed under a tree.

Actually, it looked like what school was supposed to look like. At least in the movies. At least to Jen. Her school at home was a trio of brownstones on a city block.

Jen made her way across the grass, the ground soft under her mules. She couldn't quite shake the feeling that she was on a stage set. A set where everything and everyone was new to her. She felt vaguely removed. The whole fact of her being here seemed unreal. She climbed the steps up to the main door and blinked as she went from the bright sunshine to the fluorescently lit entranceway of Capeside High.

The bank of lockers was at the end of a crowded corridor. Jen made her way down it, searching for a familiar face. That meant Dawson. Or Joey. Or that Pacey character. But she didn't spot any of them. She located her locker, number 167, top row. Spinning the dial, she worked the combination. Opened the locker. Not that she had anything to put in it yet.

She found her schedule in her bag, pulled it out, and studied it nervously: bio, English, study hall.

"Hi!" A girl with blond curls and bright lipstick came right up to her. "I'm Nellie Olson."

Jen did a double take. "Nellie Olson? As in . . ."

"I know. I know," Nellie Olson said. *"Little House on the Prairie* was, like, my mom and dad's favorite show. But no preconceptions, okay? I'm not like her at all."

35

Whatever. "Hi, I'm Jen."

"From New York City. I know. How's your grandfather? He has us all worried," Nellie said with overwrought concern. "We've still got him on the prayer list at church. You party?"

"Excuse me?" From church prayer to partying without a breath?

"Par-ty," Nellie enunciated.

Yeah, Jen had heard her right. She tried to play it cool. "As in Do I enjoy a good time? Or party as in drink-and-use-drugs party?"

"It's subjective." Nellie sounded pleased by her own observation.

"I like to have a good time, substance-free," Jen added. That was as far as she needed to go.

Nellie looked disappointed. "Maybe we should call *you* Nellie. See ya." She took off down the hall, just as Dawson was pulling up. Jen looked after her with a little frown.

"Hey, how's it going?" Dawson asked.

"I need a cigarette," Jen said without thinking.

"Do you smoke?" Dawson sounded surprised.

"I quit," Jen said quickly. "Just a little tense."

"You're hiding it well." Dawson smiled at her.

"I have a great denial system," Jen said honestly, though hooking up with somebody she knew was making her feel much less like a stray.

"It's the first day," Dawson said. "We're all tense. It'll get easier."

The guy was sweet, whatever was going on between him and Joey.

36

"How's your schedule?" he asked. "They screwed mine up. Who do you have first period?"

Jen glanced at the paper in her hand, though she'd already looked at it often enough to know it by heart. Dawson came around and looked with her. A couple of guys racing past jostled him, and he moved closer to her.

"Brinson—biology," Jen said, feeling Dawson next to her.

"I was just heading that way," Dawson said.

Jen shut her locker. "Were you?" She looked up at him and smiled. She was glad to have company as she headed down the hall.

Pacey was goofing around at the front of the classroom. The seats were about half full, and more kids were streaming in. Most of them didn't pay much attention as Pacey selected the biggest book he could find, and balanced it on his head.

All of a sudden, *she* was walking through the classroom door. No way. He had to be seeing things. Tamara! In school! But if she was a hallucination, a fantasy, she was a degree or two more buttoned up than she'd been the day before. He blinked. She was still there, in a satiny white blouse and camel-colored skirt that almost reached her knees, her curves visible, but not quite so much bare skin.

Pacey felt the *Webster's* slip. It hit the floor loudly. "Tamara?" he managed.

She smiled at him. Also a couple of degrees more proper. And then she was heading for the big desk at the front of the room, putting a stack of books down on it. "Hello, Pacey. I'll tell you what. Why don't you call me Miss Jacobs during school hours?"

Jacobs? Pacey was sure his jaw was down on the floor next to that dictionary. First period English— Miss Jacobs. "Yeah, sure . . . of course," he said.

He wasn't sure how he got to his seat. He held Tamara—Miss Jacobs—in his gaze. She was it. Even in her camel-colored skirt. Just more to imagine taking off.

Taking off? Hit that Pause button. This Mrs. Robinson was his English teacher! Pacey watched her shuffle some papers and get ready for class. Unbelievable. This wasn't happening.

Well, he'd get to see her every morning. First thing to start the day right. And she was looking for romance. She'd said it. To him.

Joey sat at her desk, doodling in her notebook and waiting for Brinson to show. High school. Not so different. School was school, basically. Lots of the same faces. Capeside's living version of Barbie and Ken sitting next to each other up front there. Joey had gone to school with both of them for years. Destined to marry and have a bunch of kids and get divorced, all by age thirty. And Marla Adams had just come through the door. And . . . Jen. Miss Neighbor. Right behind Marla.

Joey slumped down in her chair, but it was too late. Jen was smiling at her. Coming over.

"Hi. I was hoping we'd have a class together," Jen said sweetly, sliding into the seat next to Joey.

"Here we are," Joey said tonelessly. She wished the second bell would ring.

*Chapter 5*

Quietly, Dawson let himself into Mr. Gold's class-room. The teacher was up at the front of the room, sitting alone at a large video monitor, the rows of tables and chairs in back of him unoccupied.

On the screen, in vintage black-and-white, a woman was letting herself into a room, too. Vera Miles. Dawson recognized the scene instantly. Cut to a withered, dead-still figure seated in an arm-chair, white hair in a bun.

"Mrs. Bates?" Vera Miles asked, with hushed worry.

Dawson came up behind Mr. Gold. *"Psycho."*

Mr. Gold spun around, startled.

On the monitor, Vera Miles spun Mrs. Bates around to reveal a decomposing skull.

Mr. Gold looked at Dawson. "You know the film?"

Did he know the film? "Please. Anthony Perkins. Janet Leigh. 1960." Who could not know? "One of Hitchcock's most celebrated works. Little known fact: in the shower scene, Hitchcock surprised Janet Leigh with freezing cold water in order to get her to scream so effectively."

Mr. Gold arched an eyebrow. "Did you know that the fake blood used was actually—"

"Chocolate syrup," Dawson finished.

Mr. Gold took a good look at him. "Who are you?"

"Dawson Leery. Film auteur."

Mr. Gold gave a little smile. "So I take it you'll be in my fifth period film lab?"

"Actually, that's why I'm here. There seems to have been some confusion about my schedule. I was denied admittance to your class." Dawson felt irritated all over again. Most important thing on his schedule, and they'd managed to mess it up.

"Then you must be a sophomore," Mr. Gold stated.

"And that's not a good thing?" On the monitor, Vera Miles was giving a silent scream of bloody murder.

"This is a very popular class," Mr. Gold explained. "Seating is limited. There's a waiting list. Priority goes to upperclassmen."

The irritation swelled. "That's stupid," Dawson blurted.

"Excuse me?" Mr. Gold was irritated too.

"Who made that rule?" Dawson demanded.

"I did. It was the only fair way to do it."

Oops. "Oh . . ." Dawson said. But he wasn't about to give up. He'd heard that Ben Gold was a fair and decent guy. Maybe a little buttoned up—shirt and tie, chinos, glasses around his neck on a chain, shiny loafers—but, hey, he was part of the brotherhood of film. "Well, have you ever considered a screening process—an audition of sorts—thereby guaranteeing the best possible candidates?"

"Why are you so insistent?" Mr. Gold asked mildly.

"Passion, Mr. Gold. Pure, mad, driven passion. Movies are my life."

"Oh, I see." Mr. Gold eyed the death's-head on the screen.

"Sorry, I'm not coming across well at all here," Dawson said, changing tacks. "The point is, I'm going to be a filmmaker. It's my life's ambition. It always has been. How many students in your class can say that?"

Well, maybe that wasn't such a great question. Didn't everyone want to make movies? Dawson forged ahead quickly. "This is a small town. There's not a lot of opportunity for me. You have the power. You can easily override this bizarre rule that denies students their education."

Ben Gold leaned back in his chair. "You're very convincing, Dawson Leery, but I'm afraid the class is maxed out. I wish I could make case-by-case exceptions, but that would be unfair and problematic. I'm sorry, but no is my definitive answer."

Dawson wasn't hearing this. "But—"

Mr. Gold gave a small frown. "No—period. It's a complete sentence."

Dawson felt a stab of anger. Hurt. Brotherhood of film? Under those shiny loafers lay the feet of a despot.

Jen again. Joey walked down the hallway briskly, but Jen caught up with her and fell into stride. Joey didn't look at her, but this didn't seem to discourage Jen.

"Hey!" she said lightly.

"Hey!" Joey tossed back without as much enthusiasm.

"Joey? Can I ask you something important?"

Did she have a choice? "Sure." Joey kept walking, and Jen kept walking with her.

"Are you and Dawson a thing?" Jen asked.

Thing? Thang? Of course that was Jen's question. Joey was tempted to lie. Keep Jen away. But of course she and Dawson weren't a thang. Or rather they were, in a different way, but not the kind of way Jen was asking about.

"No. Not at all," Joey said, as if it was a silly idea. "We're just friends."

"Like you and I are going to be, I hope," Jen said earnestly.

Joey was silent. Why was the girl trying so hard?

But Jen was tenacious. "You know, Grams warned me about you," she said lightly. "She says you're severely troubled."

Grams. That brittle relic who seemed to get a real high out of watching Joey climb the ladder into

Dawson's room. She must have given Jen an earful. "Well, no offense, but your grams is cracked," Joey said.

"Why does she rag on you?" Jen wanted to know.

"Pick a topic. There's my dad, the imprisoned convict, and there's my sister, impregnated by her black boyfriend . . ." Joey started ticking off the facts of her life.

"Your father's in prison?" Jen sounded genuinely startled.

"Conspiracy to traffic marijuana in excess of ten thousand pounds," Joey recited.

"Wow," Jen said nonjudgmentally. "And where's your mom?"

Joey felt a tug of emotion. She resisted it. She wasn't going to let it rip her open. Not here. Not with Jen. "She had this cancer thing," Joey said flippantly. "It got her."

And that got Jen. Joey could tell. Jen didn't say anything for a few seconds. Fine. Then she asked, "So you live with your sister?"

"And her black boyfriend. He likes you, you know."

"Who, the black boyfriend?"

Enough of this. "Dawson," Joey said. She stopped walking and turned to Jen. "Don't abuse his feelings," she ordered.

She turned and walked away. She could feel Jen staring after her. The girl had better listen. This time Jen didn't follow her.

*Chapter 6*

The lunchroom was packed. First day of school and you could already see how things were divided up around Capeside High. Jocks over on one side, major food fight under way; prom queens nearby, doing carrots and celery sticks they'd brought from home; burnouts slipping out the side door.

Joey picked at her franks and beans. Boiled and steamed to death. Listening to the Dawson and Jen show didn't help. Dawson was pointing people out and commenting on them. He stabbed his plastic fork at a short, hair-impaired teacher who was walking by.

"The bald man is Mr. Herman—teaches a timid calculus but packs a forty-five magnum. Opened fire last year, took out two students and a custodian."

"Pleaded justifiable homicide. They didn't have a hall pass." Jen was quick with a comeback.

"See that girl in the funky black dress?" Dawson picked out his next victim. "Periodic drinker. Blacks out after two glasses of cheap wine and runs through town with her dress over her head—"

"Singing Neil Diamond songs," Jen finished.

Back to you, Dawson, Joey thought sourly.

"You're good," Dawson told Jen. "I should bring you in to punch up my dialogue."

Joey picked up the script that lay in front of her on the table. "We're supposed to be working, Dawson?"

Dawson flashed her a "whatever" face. "Yeah, sure." He plucked the script out of her hand. Then he turned right back to Jen. "Hey, Jen, will you take a look at my third act? I'm having a climax issue."

Climax issue. Nothing like having a way with words. Joey's face burned. So much for lunch.


Pacey found her in her classroom by herself, finishing a yogurt and a bowl of fruit salad.

"Hi, Tamara—whoops—Miss Jacobs," he said obviously.

Tamara stifled a little laugh. "Hello, Pacey."

He felt himself go weak. But not too weak to quit. "How was *The Graduate*?"

"Just as I remembered it," Tamara said.

"Looking for romance tonight?" Pacey asked smoothly. Tamara's eyes seemed to widen just a bit. Nicely done. Pacey had practiced the line in his head, but he was a little surprised at how silkenly it had slipped out.

"Why?" Tamara was looking at him—that way. "Do you have any suggestions?" she said teasingly.

Down, boy. *"Summer of '42?"* he said, trying to stay cool.

"Refresh my memory." She leaned back in her chair and gave Pacey her full attention.

"It's about this beautiful woman who seduces a young boy on the verge of manhood."

Tamara stared at him. She raised one perfectly arched eyebrow. "It's a favorite," she said in a low voice.

I am your slave, Miss Jacobs. Pacey felt himself starting to sweat. "I can reserve it for you if you'd like," he said.

One of Tamara's students entered the room. A tall, skinny guy in a green watch cap. He was followed by a petite blond girl. Wet shower. Tamara sat upright in her chair. "Actually, tonight I'm going to see that new film playing at the Rialto." She took a last bite of yogurt.

"Yeah?" Pacey said, trying not to let the moment get away.

More students began to stream in. Some kids Pacey knew. That guy from the hockey team who'd just rented *Scream*. Pacey knew it was over.

"It's getting great reviews," Tamara commented— easily, suggestively.

"Oh yeah? Then I'll have to check it out," Pacey said. Maybe it *wasn't* over.

Pacey looked as if he'd done a couple of laps around the track in his street clothes, Dawson thought. He was breathing hard. His face was flushed. There was a line of moisture over his upper lip.

"Easy," Dawson said as Pacey caught up to him in the hall near the lockers.

"Check it out," Pacey commanded. "Video Woman is my new English teacher."

Video Woman? Dawson looked at Pacey's red cheeks. Wildman eyes. The woman from yesterday? An English teacher at Capeside High?

"Right, dude," Pacey confirmed, reading Dawson's expression. "So you and me—the movies. Tonight. We're stalking a faculty member."

"Negative," Dawson said immediately. He wasn't getting anywhere near Pacey's dream life. Anyway, he had his own.

Pacey jostled his arm. "Man, I actually have the possibility of losing my virginity in high-level fantasy fashion."

"Pacey, go home. Walk your dog. It's not gonna happen with the English teacher." Dawson stopped at the water fountain and took a drink.

"Not tonight," Pacey actually agreed. "That's not the plan."

Oh, no. Not a *plan*.

"I just wanna establish my presence," Pacey went on. "So she can start to become familiar with my smile, gaze, and other charming features."

"Don't do this to yourself," Dawson advised Pacey.

"It is a fact that a large percentage of older women are attracted to young boys on the verge of

manhood. It keeps them feeling young. I read it in
*Cosmopolitan.*"

*Cosmopolitan*? Pacey was sicker than he'd
thought. "What are you doing reading—"

"I have three menstrually diverse sisters. *Cosmo*
is my salvation."

"So what do you need me for?" Dawson asked.

"Moral support. It'll be cool. You can invite Miss
Teen New York," Pacey added. He looked down
toward the bank of lockers. "Unless someone's
beating you to it."

Dawson followed Pacey's gaze. Jen. Talking to
Roger Fulford. Jen, her back against the lockers,
kind of leaning into them with her shoulders and
looking up at that swell-chested, towheaded slab of
beef. Roger was standing just a little too close to
her. The alligator Dawson knew was on Roger's
shirt, under his letter jacket, was almost near
enough to take a drink from her pale blue sweater.
And he makes the pass.

Dawson felt Pacey give him a push toward Jen
and Roger. "Get over there. Intercept, Dawson.
Make it happen. Be assertive. Women like that. You
should start reading *Cosmopolitan*. It'll build your
female esteem," he coached, laughing.

Dawson ignored Pacey. Roger was moving away.
Dawson moved in.

Jen looked over and saw him coming. "Hey, Dawson. How's it going?"

"I see you met Roger Fulford," Dawson noted.

"Nice guy," Jen said easily.

"Sure. Jock by day, schizophrenic transvestite by night," Dawson informed her.

"Really?" Jen laughed. They started walking down the hall together, leaving Pacey somewhere back in the Capeside High nebula.

"Has what you would call a Tori Spelling complex," Dawson went on, still describing Roger. "Partial to Victoria's Secret. Just so you know." Roger Fulford in a deep green satin push-up bra and matching panties.

"But can he run in pumps?" Jen winged back.

They were on a roll. No time like right now. "Hey, Pacey is cruise-directing a trip to the movies tonight," Dawson said. "Just a few of us. Nothing big. Would you like to come?" Easy. Casual.

Jen smiled at him just as easily and casually. "Sure," she said.

"Hey, I need a favor," Dawson called out to Joey as she walked home from school via the scenic route, along the harbor.

"Uh-oh." Joey looked at him and rolled her eyes.

"I have a semi-quasi date with Jen tonight. We're going to the movies with Pacey, and I need you to come with us."

"I'd rather go down in a plane crash."

"Come on! It'll be really weird, just two guys and Jen. You would even it out."

"So it would look like a double date?" Joey said, with a bad taste in her mouth.

"Sorta . . . but not really. Pacey's on this hormonal mission."

Pacey's hormones. This got better and better. Not. "Have you had an aneurysm?" Joey asked. "No way!"

"It's not a *date*-date," Dawson said pleadingly. "It's just so Jen won't be uncomfortable."

"We wouldn't want that," Joey said pointedly, letting the last word of her sentence rip like an arrow.

Dawson passed on that one. "Come on, Joe, please. Please, please, please, please, please."

Joey listened to him repeat the word until it dissolved into meaninglessness.

"Please, please, please . . ."

She stifled a small smile.

"Please, please, please, please . . ."

He wasn't going to stop. "Oh, whatever," she finally said. Dawson wanted her to do this for him. He was dying for her to do this. It was a couple of hours in her life.

He pounced on her and wrapped her in a hug. Not a tender, thang kind of hug. A friends, slap-on-the-back, guy kind of hug. "You're the best," he told her. "I mean it. I know you've been worried about our relationship and everything, but I told you nothing has to change. See? We can talk about anything."

Joey stared at him. Talk? Dawson had begged. She'd given in. When was he going to get his head out of the celluloid and grow up?

*Chapter 7*

Jen fastened the clasp on her locket chain as she came into the kitchen. Grams was preparing a bowl of egg salad, neatly chopping celery and onions to add to the eggs. As Jen entered the room, Grams paused, knife in midair as she fixed her gaze on her granddaughter. Jen saw her make a swift inventory of her outfit—blue floral-print dress, pale green sweater, sandals, a touch of makeup.

"Where exactly are you going?" her grandmother asked softly.

But under the softness was a demand. Jen felt a flicker of defensiveness. "Well . . . Dawson has a gun, and we thought we'd knock over a few liquor stores and then go for some tattoos," she said sweetly.

Her grandmother gave a distressed little laugh. "Why do you talk like that, dear?"

"I'm simply trying to establish a rapport with you, Grams, that's based on humor." It was the truth, more or less. That and she needed to let at least a little of her personality roam free. "I'm completely harmless," she added. "You'll see."

Grams didn't rise to the challenge. "Well, just be home by ten," she said.

"I can do that," Jen assured her. "Thanks for being so cool about this. I was a little worried you were going to chain me to a chair or something." She *was* relieved that Grams wasn't giving her a hard time about going out. "We're going to the movies," she added.

"Fine," her grandmother said. "You want to go to the movies, go. Have fun. As long as you come to church with me on Sunday."

Oh, that. "I should've known there was a catch. Look, Grams, I'm sorry, but you're gonna have to give up on that."

"I'm afraid I insist." There was forged steel under her pleasantness.

Jen took a deep breath. The face-off. This was about respect—Jen respecting herself. Expecting others to respect her, too. Grams included. "I'm firm about my beliefs, Grams. Please respect them."

Grams looked at Jen. "I know what happened in New York. *Church*"—she emphasized the word—"will do you good."

Go easy, Jen told herself. Easy but strong. She was ready to go forward without letting mistakes from the past pull her back. "Let me determine that, Grams. Church isn't the answer. Not for me. But I promise you I'll keep an open mind and respect and honor your beliefs as long as I'm here." Truth.

Her grandmother didn't budge. "The decision has been made. You're under my guard. You'll do what I say." Even the appearance of softness was gone from her voice now.

Jen felt her cheeks getting hot. "I'm really trying hard to keep my rebellious nature in check." She gave a forced laugh. "I'll tell you what, Grams. I'll go to church when you say the word 'penis.' "

Grams looked as though someone had dropped a bomb on her house. The knife fell to the table with a clatter. Jen actually felt a drop of pity for her. But she'd tried the considerate approach and it seemed as if her grandmother just couldn't hear her.

"You stop that talk," her grandmother ordered.

"It's just a word, Grams. Technical and clinical. 'Penis.' " And before Grams could muster a response, Jen leaned over and delivered a peremptory kiss to her cheek. "Grams, I really love you but you gotta lighten up." No lie.

Her grandmother looked as if she wondered what she'd gotten into. To that and only that, Jen related entirely.

"See ya later." She pushed open the rear screen door and sailed out into the mellow late afternoon.

Grams didn't make any move to stop her. But Jen knew that didn't mean she'd won.

When Dawson came downstairs to say good-bye, his dad was sweating over his restaurant model again. Across the room the TV was on. A tissue-thin, purple-inked architectural drawing was spread out over his desk. On top of it sat a miniature three-dimensional model of a building, all curved walls and undulating surfaces, rooms stuffed with dolls and tiny plastic fish, nautical decorations, and who knew what else. You could get seasick looking at it. Welcome to the dollhouse, Dad.

"I'm outta here," Dawson announced, pulling a light sweater over his head. "See ya, Dad."

His father held up one of the dolls. "What do you think?" She was wearing a scuba suit. "I thought all the waitresses should wear scuba gear."

"Completely impractical," Dawson said frankly. "You know, Dad, this whole aquatic-theme restaurant idea gets worse on a daily basis."

His father just craned his head as if to look past Dawson. "Shift," he said. "It's your mom. She's doing her oil spill exclusive."

Dawson turned toward the television. His mom was on screen with her serious face.

"Watching her work is the best foreplay," Dawson's father said.

"Thank you for sharing that with me, Dad. "I'm outta here," Dawson told him again, already half-way out of the room.

"Have fun," his father said. "Play safe."

Dawson stopped. He wished his dad would. "The condom chat is premature, Dad."

"It's never too early, son."

Dawson rolled his eyes. "What is up with the sex? That's all anybody thinks about anymore. Sex, sex,

sex. Why is our society so immersed in sex? What is the big deal?"

"Sex is a very big part of who we are as human beings," Mr. Leery lectured.

Thank you, Dr. Ruth. Dawson had heard more than enough. "Does that mean we have to roll all over the coffee table? C'mon, if sex is so important, how come Spielberg has never had a sex scene in one of his movies? Huh? He keeps it in its proper place in film. As we should in life."

The doorbell sounded throughout the house. Jen! Dawson was moving again. "I'll be home early."

He didn't like his father's superior smile.

As he left the room, he heard his mother's voice. "Back to you, Bob."


Ready for battle. Joey pulled on a tan work shirt over her T-shirt, brushed an imaginary speck of dirt off her white jeans, and pushed through the screen door. Bess was out on the porch, painting the wooden trim of their home. Smudges of rich oil paint streaked the smock she had on over a pretty cotton dress, and the scent of turpentine mingled with the salty-sulfur smell of low tide. Bodie lay on the porch couch next to Bess, studying some recipe in *Bon Appétit*. Jazz tunes floated out of the house. Ah, the perfect picture of tranquil domesticity. Yeah, right.

Joey raced past them. Tried to. But Bess caught her by her shirt. "Whoa. Where are you going?"

"I'm in a huge hurry," Joey said. The last thing she needed to start this fabulous evening off was an encounter with her sister.

"Your attitude has got to go," Bess said.

Joey felt her neck muscles clench. She strained to get free, but Bess grabbed her face in one hand and squeezed her cheeks together. Joey's mouth went into an involuntary pucker. Kiss of death. "Ouch!" she protested.

Bess plunged her free hand into her smock pocket and came up with a slender black-and-gold tube of lipstick. With her mouth, she managed to pop the top off and, with one hand, expertly swivel the deep red stick up. Joey felt her sister's hold ease. She aimed the lipstick at Joey's lips and carefully applied the color.

Joey was caught totally off guard. She'd been preparing for the usual war. She felt a queasy flutter of confusion.

Bodie glanced at them and smiled approvingly.

Bess let go of Joey's face. "Now blot 'em together like this." She pressed her own full, pretty lips together and moved them from side to side.

Joey obeyed automatically.

Bess swiveled the lipstick back down and closed it. She pressed it into Joey's hand. "You hold on to this, and every half hour to an hour you excuse yourself for a touch-up. Got it?"

For once, Joey had no snappy answer. Joey felt a funny little ache at her sister's tenderness, and she didn't know what to do about it. Stuffing the lipstick into a pocket of her work shirt, she took off across the front lawn. Then, without overthinking it, she stopped, turned, and gave Bess a genuine smile.

Bess smiled back, just as genuinely.

## Chapter 8

Joey was stuck with Pacey, bringing up the rear of their little foursome. Dawson and Jen walked in front, weaving through the evening crowd. The weather was beautiful, and tonight there seemed to be a lot of people in town for September—doing a little late shopping before the stores closed, heading into one of the restaurants, taking the kids out for an ice-cream cone, or just enjoying an evening stroll on Main Street.

"So, do you plan on staying the whole school year?" Dawson was asking Jen.

Good question, Joey thought.

"Well, that all depends on my grandfather. And my mom and dad." There was a note of uncertainty in Jen's voice. "I don't know." She shrugged uncomfortably. Then she turned around toward Joey

57

and gave a hesitant smile, as if to invite her into the conversation. "I love your lipstick, Joey. What shade is it?"

Joey started to smile without meaning to. Then she saw Dawson look at her mouth. She felt a wave of embarrassment. Thanks a lot, Jen. "Wicked Red. I like your hair color. What number is it?"

Dawson glared at her. "You'll have to excuse Joey. She was born in a barn."

And thank you, too, Dawson Leery.

"That's okay," Jen said quickly. "Joey, I only do highlights."

So sweet. So forthright. Didn't anything rattle Jen? "So, Jen, are you a virgin?" Joey asked.

Jen gave a strangled little sound halfway between a cough and a choke.

Got you.

Dawson's mouth dropped open. "That's mature," he said disgustedly.

Joey couldn't seem to stop. It was as if her words were taking on a life of their own. "Because Dawson is a virgin, and two virgins really makes for a clumsy first encounter. Don't you think?"

"You're gonna die," Dawson threatened. "Painfully."

"I just thought I'd help," Joey said extra sweetly. "You know, cut to the chase." The marquee of the Rialto was right in front of them, spelling out their movie: *Waiting for Guffman*.

"It's okay, Dawson." Jen saved the day again. "Yes, I'm a virgin. How about you, Joey? Are you?"

Joey wasn't ready for that one. Jen might be sweet

and unflappable, but she was also quick. "Please," Joey said, trying to come up with something fast. "Years ago. Trucker named Bubba." She moved toward the ticket window.

Dawson grabbed her arm. "What is up with you?" he whispered roughly.

They bought their tickets and headed in. Joey wasn't really sure she could have answered Dawson's question even if she'd wanted to. Jen was genuinely nice—and trying way harder than Joey deserved. But still . . .

Pacey led the way, finding four seats in a row about halfway back. Joey followed him in, Dawson behind her, but as she moved toward her seat, Dawson stopped in the aisle and let Jen go ahead of him. Well, chivalry was alive and well in Capeside. Which meant that Joey got stuck between Jen and Pacey.

She slumped down in her seat. All of a sudden Pacey shot to his feet again. "Back in a bit," he said cryptically, then hurried up toward one of the front rows.

And thank you, too, Pacey. Now it was just Dawson and Jen and Joey. Nothing quite like a trio. The lights dimmed. Joey sneaked a look over at Dawson. His hand hovered on the armrest between him and Jen. He drummed his fingers nervously. Jen's hand was on her leg—the one closest to Dawson, of course. Joey pursed her lips. Dawson shifted, leaning toward Jen. His hand started inching over. Stopped. Started again. Going, going . . .

"So, Jen," Joey found herself saying. "You a size queen?"

"Excuse me?" Jen asked.

"How important is the size to you?"

"Joey!" Dawson was shooting major bullets at her with his eyes.

Jen fixed Joey with a level gaze, as if considering what to say. "Being a virgin, I haven't given it much thought." Was that a note of weariness creeping in her voice? Was Miss Gung Ho Camper starting to get tired of their little game? But Jen kept playing stoically, turning Joey's question back at her. "How about you?" she asked Joey.

"I'm torn—" Joey managed to say, before Dawson yanked her out of her seat.

"You and me. Outside. Now."

"What do *you* think, Dawson?" Joey asked loudly.

"I'm gonna kill you," Dawson growled. "Kill you dead."

The opening credits were rolling. "Shhh," said someone in the next row.

Dawson was pulling Joey out into the aisle. She looked back over her shoulder at Jen and got in one last line. "Did you notice the long fingers?" she asked.

Dawson dragged Joey up the aisle and out of the theater.

Pacey plopped down in the empty seat next to Tamara. "Hi, Tamara."

She looked at him, and her face colored with surprise. "Pacey! What are you doing here?"

Well, she'd basically invited him. "I came to check out the movie, like you suggested," Pacey said. "I'm here with some friends."

Tamara's surprise melted into a smile. "Some friends? Oh, I'm glad."

"But I can sit with you, if you like. Milk Duds?" He held out the box.

"No," Tamara said. She shifted around in her seat. Hadn't her shirt been buttoned up one button farther in school, today?

"Oh, *Summer of '42* is officially reserved in your name," Pacey told her.

"Oh, Pacey, I don't think you understand."

"It was no problem," Pacey said quickly. He was trying to get up the nerve to suggest they watch it together, when some middle-aged guy entered their row—shirt and tie, chinos, glasses on a chain around his neck, shiny loafers. He carried a barrel-size tub of popcorn.

"Ah, Pacey, are you sure you don't want to sit with your friends?" Tamara asked. She looked from him to the popcorn dude.

Pacey gave him a second look too. Enough popcorn for two. At least. And then some. Heading right this way. Suddenly Pacey got a bad feeling. "Who's this guy?" he asked Tamara.

"Tammy, is this kid bothering you?" the man asked.

"Shhh!" said a guy behind them as the lights dimmed.

"No, Benji," Tamara said.

"*Benji?* Miss Jacobs invited me herself," Pacey clarified.

"Not exactly, Pacey, but I . . . can see how . . ." Tamara stumbled over her words.

Pacey felt a sudden flicker of insecurity.

"Why don't I help you find a seat?" the Benji character said. It was more of a statement than an offer. He reached for Pacey's arm.

"*Shh!*" the guy behind them hissed.

Pacey yanked his arm away. Benji staggered. The popcorn went flying. Suddenly the guy behind them was covered with it. Buried in the blizzard.

"What the—" He stood up menacingly.

He was huge. It was the last thing Pacey noticed, before a meaty fist came sailing toward his face.

Joey and Dawson stood in the lobby of the theater, arguing, their voices loud enough to provide a show for the refreshment vendors and ticket takers.

"Are you tweakin'?" Dawson shouted. "What is your problem?"

"My problem is that from the moment little Miss Highlights showed up you haven't said one word to me," Joey shouted back.

"Crap!" Dawson hurled the word. "That is pure crap and you know it."

"What I know is that all your blood is rushing downward and you can't acknowledge that another human being is present."

"I like her, okay? Sue me. I thought you were my

friend." Dawson frowned deeply. "Where's a little understanding?"

"I understand everything," Joey said. "I'm tired of understanding." And all of a sudden she *felt* tired. Really tired. "All I do is understand." She felt a tear settle in the corner of her eye.

Dawson took a long look at her. "Joey—"

"Nothing penetrates with you." Joey blinked hard against the tear. "You're so far removed from reality you don't see what's right in front of you."

"What are you talking about?" Dawson was yelling again.

"Your life, Dawson. It's a friggin' fairy tale, and you don't even know it. You just want conflict for that script you're writing in your head." Dawson's world. Joey was sick of it. "Stop living in the movies. Grow up!"

# Chapter 9

The creek was bathed in moonlight. The Big Dipper sparkled crisply in the velvet sky. The first spicy-sweet note of fall rode a gentle breeze. Way in the distance, you could hear the surf.

Dawson and Jen headed slowly across her grandparents' front lawn.

"I'll walk you to your door," Dawson said.

Jen shook her head. "Not with Grams ready to pounce."

Dawson glanced toward her darkened porch. "Oh, that's right."

They stopped walking. "So . . ." he said.

She gave a soft laugh. "So . . ."

"It was . . ." Dawson groped for the right thing to say. "It was a really repulsive evening."

Jen's laugh opened up. "Yeah," she said. "Yeah, it was."

Dawson laughed too. There was a wordless moment. Wind through the trees. A bird chirping. They both stopped walking. Dawson looked at her. She was looking at him. Eyes bright. Hair shining, the color of moonlight. Dawson's heart was pounding. She was beautiful. And sweet. And smart. And fun to be with. He moved closer.

She tilted her face up toward his. He could smell the floral scent of her shampoo. He put his hand on her arm, felt an electricity go through him as he touched her. He leaned in toward her, his lips close to hers—

Suddenly she turned her face away. "This is all my fault," Jen said.

Dawson felt a jolt of disappointment. Her fault? A kiss?

"I know I don't possess much power in the universe, but I feel completely responsible for tonight," she explained.

She thought it was *her* fault? Joey goes ballistic. Pacey winds up on the floor of the theater. *His* two friends. And it's her fault?

"No, it's me," Dawson protested. "I pulled the pin. I tossed the grenade. I have this big *L* embedded right here." He made an *L* with his fingers and brought it to his forehead.

Jen shook her head. "No. You're not a loser, Dawson. I think you're very sweet and smart. And you have a great sense of humor."

Dawson felt an embarrassed grin starting to happen. But Jen wasn't finished.

"You're cool without being obnoxious about it. You're very, very talented."

"Yeah?" Dawson laughed softly. What had he done to deserve this?

"Yeah. And have clear skin. A big plus."

He laughed louder. The laugh faded, and he felt even more nervous than he'd been a few moments earlier. "Thank you," he said.

"No. Thank *you*. Things weren't so great for me in New York," Jen told him. "And, well . . . things are really scary for me right now, too." She glanced briefly at her grandparents' house.

Jen somehow seemed strong and fragile at the same time. Dawson pressed his palm against her face. Her skin was soft. Warm. They held each other's gaze. She didn't pull away. He leaned in for the kiss.

The porch lights snapped on. They both looked toward the house. Dawson could see Jen's grandmother standing just inside the door, peering out.

Jen took a step away from him. "I have to go," she said reluctantly. "Thanks for everything, Dawson."

"But—" he said to her back as she ran up the flagstone walkway. He felt his hope escaping with her.

Suddenly she turned back. "I'm just gonna pretend we kissed, Dawson, okay?"

Dawson grinned. Yeah. More than okay. He was going to pretend he'd kissed Jen, too.

\* \* \*

66

Pacey could feel the dried blood, tight and brittle, on his face. One eye was swollen nearly shut, functional but throbbing. He wandered aimlessly down by the harbor, unable to bear the thought of going home, getting into bed, and being alone with his humiliation. Not that he was doing much of a job of getting away from it here. But at least he could delay having to explain his swollen eye to his parents or sisters or brother.

He ambled toward the area where the pleasure boats were docked. A half-dozen or so salt-darkened walkways were suspended over the water on solid wood piles. Yachts and elegant sailboats were berthed in neat rows. Many were dark, but there were signs of life on a few of them. A lamp burned in a sleek, well-appointed cabin. He saw the gray-purple glow of a television in another. A few people still sat up on deck here and there, enjoying the mild night.

Pacey picked a row at random and headed out toward the end of the boardwalk. He'd win the Fool of the Decade Award, for sure. Coming on all Romeo to some way seasoned Juliet. Except she wasn't Juliet. She was his English teacher. That's Miss Jacobs, to you. And he'd gotten so deep into fantasyland that he'd provided the dramatic high point of the week. Maybe the year. Pathos, violence, and comedy all rolled up in some stranger's fist on his face.

Of course it wasn't totally his fault. "I'm in the mood for romance," she'd said. "Where would I find *The Graduate*?" And how about *"Summer of*

'42 . . . ? It's a favorite." She had to know how that came off to a boy his age. And she'd said it anyway. Said it on purpose.

And suddenly there she was, like a mirage. Appearing in the moonlight and the lights from the harbor. Except he wasn't just imagining her this time. Tamara—Miss Jacobs—was standing at the end of the pier, looking out at the water with a troubled expression. The warm silver of the moon shone on her face, which was even more beautiful for her look of melancholy.

Pacey was hit with a mixture of fury and desire. He felt sick. And Tamara had spotted him. "Great. What are the chances?" he mumbled.

"Pacey, are you okay?" All full of concern.

"I'll live." Why was he talking to her? Hadn't tonight taught him anything? He turned to beat a retreat.

She caught up to him and reached for his arm. "Wait, Pacey. Talk to me a second."

Pacey felt her touch, all sensory input focused overtime on her hand. It just sharpened his anger. "About what? *The Graduate* or *Summer of '42*? Which would you rather discuss?"

"I'd like to clear up this misunderstanding," she said sincerely. Her hand was still on his arm.

Pacey shook it off. "I understand you perfectly well . . . Miss Jacobs," he added for emphasis.

"I'm so sorry," Tamara said simply.

"You should be, because you're a liar. How can you say you were only renting a movie?" Pacey felt his anger gathering momentum—a giant wave.

"Because it's the truth." Tamara actually sounded as if she believed that. And *Summer of '42*? The favorite? Just a casual comment?

"What a crock!" The wave of anger was rolling. "The truth is you're a well-put-together knockout of a woman who's feeling a little insecure about hitting forty. So when a young, virile boy such as myself flirts with you, you enjoy it. You encourage it. You even fantasize about what it would be like to be with that young boy on the verge of manhood." Pacey let it rip, and it felt good. "Because it helps you stay feeling attractive and makes the aging process a little more bearable. Well, let me tell you something. You blew it, lady. Because I'm the best sex you'll never have!"

Whoa! Pacey needed to catch his breath. That was totally unrehearsed. Totally what he wanted to say. Tamara looked stunned. Her gaze was frozen on him. She didn't say a word.

Now what? Pacey felt the surge of strength going out of him.

"You're wrong about one thing, Pacey," Tamara said softly.

Oh, really?

"You're not a boy." She grabbed his hands and drew him toward her. Their faces were only inches apart. They came together in a heated kiss.

Pacey wrapped her in his arms, feeling her body against his. Her lips were soft. He could taste their desire.

And then she was pulling away, staring at him, stunned. "I—I'm sorry," she whispered. "Oh, God!"

Regret and shock rang in her voice. She backed away from him.

Pacey watched her go. He could barely catch his breath.

She turned away from him and broke into an awkward jog. Hit and run. Into the night. Just renting a video. Gone.

"I'll see you in school," Pacey said to her back. "Miss Jacobs."

Dawson walked into his room and grabbed the remote. Power on. Gray snow morphed into the local weatherman. "There will be some fine weather in the next few days. . . ."

Dawson picked up a crumpled shirt from his bed, packed it into a ball, and yanked open his closet for the toss.

Joey was huddled on the floor, surrounded by dirty clothes.

"Joe! What are you doing in there?"

Joey stood up, holding the E.T. doll, looking sheepish. "Hanging with the clothes."

"What happened tonight, Joey?"

Joey took a perfectly aimed dive onto the bed. She landed on her stomach. "I wigged out."

That much he knew. Dawson let his sweater drop into the bottom of his closet. "*What* is going on between us?"

Joey shook her head, her long brown hair swirling around her. Her lipstick had rubbed off. "I have no idea," she said slowly.

Dawson felt the tension between them, joining

them but keeping them apart. There had always been this unspoken communication between him and Joey. Unspoken because each knew exactly what the other one was thinking. Now there was something unspoken, and Dawson didn't know what Joey was thinking. Feeling. Or what he was feeling, either. He couldn't get this vague, constant unease in him to crystallize, to form words, to shape itself into a script.

Joey was right. He was living a movie. "I know I have this incredibly perfect life and I completely underappreciate it," he said. He didn't want Joey to be angry. Especially not at him. And he didn't want to be angry, either.

"Yeah, you do," she said.

"And I'm sorry I'm such an insensitive male. I thought I was above it." Dawson pulled out his desk chair and sat down. "I don't want to lose you, Joey." As he said it, the weight of his words sank in even deeper. "What we have is the only thing that makes any sense to me."

Joey moved her head almost imperceptibly. Was that a nod of agreement or a shake of doubt, of having had enough? For a brief moment Dawson saw a confused, pretty girl lying on his bed. Not just his old pal. And that sent a jolt of surprise through him. Surprise and honesty. It wasn't the first time he'd felt this way. Even though he'd just realized it.

"You know, when I saw you tonight with lipstick on, I remember thinking how pretty you looked," he confessed. "I ignored it," he added with a quick laugh, "but I thought it."

"Yeah?" Joey asked. She smiled.

"But that was it, Joe," Dawson said with brutal sincerity. He'd never lied to Joey. "It didn't go further than that."

She shrugged. If he'd expected her to be crushed, she didn't look it. But her casual reaction didn't surprise him, either. "When I saw you going for Jen's hand tonight, it's not like I wanted to be the one holding your hand," Joey said with equal candor. "I just didn't want her holding it."

Dawson understood her completely. For a second the confusion between them vanished. But that didn't change the situation. "So where does that leave us?" Dawson asked.

Another shrug—this one less illuminating.

"It's all so complicated," Dawson said.

"We're growing up, Dawson. That's all." Suddenly Joey had an answer. "Even Spielberg outgrew his Peter Pan syndrome." And then she was up and moving toward the window.

"Where are you going?" Dawson asked, standing automatically. But he knew it was a lame question, even as he asked it.

"I can't sleep over anymore," Joey said. Again. "And we can't talk to each other the way we used to. There are things we can't say."

Every bit of Dawson's gut emotion rebelled against her words. Maybe things had gotten more complicated between them, but hadn't they both just admitted it? Hadn't they always, always told each other everything? Dawson couldn't bear to see Joey climb out that window. It was like his right leg, a piece of him, was going out, too. "That's just not true! I can tell you anything," he insisted.

Joey fixed him with a direct gaze. "How often do you walk your dog?"

"What?" Dawson looked puzzled.

"You know what I mean," said Joey. "What time of day? How many times a week?"

It took a second for her questions to sink in. Then Dawson felt the embarrassment of his most private moments laid right out there between them. What everyone knew but what you didn't talk about to anyone. Well, actually, he'd used that dog-walking line on Pacey the other day when he was getting all sweaty about that teacher lady. But it was guy talk. Code phrasing.

Dawson looked at Joey, poised to climb out the window. The look in her eyes challenged him to answer. Begged him to answer. "Good night." It was all he could say. Joey was right. He didn't want her to be right. And he could see she didn't want to be, either. She just was.

"See ya, Dawson," she said softly. She disappeared down the side of the house.

"See ya, Joey," Dawson said to himself. He stood there for a long time. He hurt. He didn't know what he felt. He wanted life to be simple again. He was so tired. He leaned his head against the closet door. He banged his head, hard, against the door. Again. As if he could bang out all his confusion and pain.

Joey struggled with the line to her rowboat. She wiped away her tears with the back of her hand, but more welled up in her eyes. The dock was blurry, and she couldn't see why the rope in her hands had snagged. She half stood in the little boat, gave a yank, and felt the boat wobble precariously. The tears made their way down her cheeks. Why fight them? No one could see her, anyway.

She finally got the boat unmoored and started rowing. She tugged on the oars angrily. Felt good, actually, to channel her anger into a purely physical activity. The rowboat glided out into the creek. It was a beautiful night. Moon, stars. The whole bit. Not too still, not too wild. In between summer and fall. Perfect. Unfair, really. Given the circumstances.

"Hey, Joey!" Dawson's voice carried across the water.

Startled, Joey looked up toward his room. Dawson was half out of the window, waving madly. She felt a funny little flutter inside—hope, anticipation.

"Usually in the morning, with Katie Couric!" Dawson yelled.

Huh? Katie Couric? And then it hit her. When do you walk your dog? Joey felt a huge grin stretch across her face. She waved back at Dawson just as athletically. Her spirit soared. She saw that Dawson was grinning too.

Whatever they were going through, at least they were going through it together. Dawson gave one last overdone wave and disappeared back inside. Joey began to row toward home.

# Chapter 10

Joey's voice was emotional. "I know what I saw. It was big and ugly, and it attacked me. And it's still out there. Waiting."

As she sat on Dawson's bed, watching herself speak to Pacey in the dailies of Dawson's movie project, Joey was tempted to point the remote at the VCR and stop the film before she saw the next scene. She felt the corners of her mouth turn down with anticipated disgust.

"I may not believe you, Stephanie," Pacey was saying on the screen, "but I believe *in* you."

Here goes nothing. Joey watched as Pacey leaned over and kissed her movie alter ego on the mouth. As soon as his lips touched hers, she recoiled. On Dawson's bed, she felt herself pull back from thin air in horrified sympathy. On the screen, she saw herself cringe and make an exaggerated "gag me" face.

"Cut," Dawson could be heard saying on video.

"What? What?" Pacey asked defensively.

They were way off character, but the camera was still rolling.

"I'm sorry, Dawson," Joey heard her video self say, "but he's too repellent."

The picture shifted to snow.

"Joey, you're going to have to kiss him," Dawson said from the other side of the room. He sat in his desk chair, hunched over one of his latex masks, paintbrush in hand.

"I cannot and will not kiss that cretin," Joey stated.

Dawson clicked his tongue. "It's a movie. You're playing a character. It's not Pacey you're kissing."

If it looks like Pacey, if it tastes like Pacey . . .

"So he's a sea serpent from the deep. Cite the difference," Joey challenged.

"But you're not aware of his alter ego." Dawson did a quick, pointless plot summary. "You're in love with him."

"Forget it."

"The movie won't work without the kiss, Joey. It's a love story," Dawson said.

"It's a horror movie, Dawson."

"That's blasphemy! It's an homage with a heavy allegorical slant."

Just when you thought it was safe to go back to the movies.

Joey flopped onto her back on the bed, remembering the horror of Pacey's mouth diving down at her face. Eaten by the sea creature. "But he's so unkissworthy," Joey said.

"Do this for me," Dawson said.

"I don't want to regurgitate on camera. Why don't you kiss him, Dawson?"

"Because my lips are reserved for someone else." Dawson didn't miss a beat.

But Joey did. Suddenly it wasn't just a movie. She reached for a response. "What is up with that? Have you kissed Miss Someone Else yet?" Okay. Nicely tossed off. But she found herself waiting for the answer with just a little too much . . . well, interest.

"Almost," Dawson said. "The moment nears."

Wipe the smile, dude. "What's the delay?"

Dawson had to think for a moment too long. Two points to me, Joey thought. But so what?

"There's no need to rush fate," Dawson answered.

So now Jen was his fate? How dramatic. How classical. "Don't wait an eternity, Dawson. Your first date with her—such as it was—was days ago. She's from New York, where things tend to move faster."

"So how enchanting for her to meet a strapping young man who doesn't have sex on the brain." Dawson came back immediately with that one. Ooh, the pious hero.

"If it helps you sleep at night," Joey said. When was the guy going to stop living in a dream?

"You heard her yourself. By her own admission— she's a virgin."

"For another second."

"Jen happens to be a bright, intelligent young woman who is clearly in charge of her own body," Dawson said, walking on the defensive side.

Joey laughed. She hadn't meant to launch quite so direct an attack on the fantasy innocence of Dawson's daydreams. Or maybe she had. "I'm not suggesting leather straps and Crisco—just a kiss."

Dawson worked his paintbrush carefully. "Jen and I will definitely kiss. Don't you worry. The question is, will your lips ever find Pacey's?"

Oh, back to that. Back to you, Bob. "Rewrite," Joey demanded. "I vote for an extensive rewrite."

"That's too bad," Dawson said. "Because you definitely have kissable lips."

"What!" Joey sat up. She hadn't heard that.

Dawson held up the mask he was working on. A latex head, like the one Pacey wore as the sea creature. But it was definitely not a sea creature. It was her! It was Joey! How had she missed that one? And the scariest thing about this mask was how much it actually looked like her. Damn, Dawson was good.

"For the decapitation scene," Dawson said mildly. "Check out those lips. You give good lip."

Joey couldn't think of a single comeback. Did she have kissable lips? Did Dawson think so? Even though he really dreamed of kissing Miss Someone Else?

"You know, Joey, you could always just close your eyes and think of someone else." Think of Jen? Wait. He meant someone else. Not Someone Else, as in little Miss Someone Else. This was getting too confusing. All Joey knew was that she most decidedly did not want to kiss Pacey. Wasn't going to.

"You're full of solutions, Dawson." Joey flopped back down on the bed. So who was she supposed to pretend she was kissing? She glanced over at Dawson. He was studying the mask of her face, smiling, pleased with his work.

Suddenly he put it down. He looked at her. "Explain to me the Crisco?"

Joey laughed. She wasn't going to destroy Dawson's perfectly scripted innocence.

*Chapter 11*

Dawson slammed the door of his locker and threaded his way down the hall. "Hey, man," he greeted Keith Silves as they passed in the opposite directions. Hadn't seen him all summer. Probably out on his boat with his girlfriend, Marla. The hall was packed with kids racing to class before the second bell. Lots of familiar faces. Lots of new ones, too.

The loudspeaker crackled from somewhere up near the ceiling. Some kids kept going, ignoring the sound. Some stopped to listen to the disembodied voice blasting into the hall. "Good morning!"

Dawson kept walking, though for a second he thought he had been transported to Screenplay Video and that he was at work. That was Nellie's voice chasing him down the hall.

"Don't forget about the big dance on Saturday to celebrate our victory at the big game on Friday even if we don't know yet if we'll even win the big game, but the planning committee is really optimistic so get your tickets now. . . ."

Take a breath, Nell. Dawson made a right into Mr. Gold's room. The classroom was deserted, except for Ben Gold himself, fiddling with some camera equipment in the back of the room.

Dawson knocked on the inside of the door. "Mr. Gold. Got a sec?"

Ben Gold looked up, bringing his glasses to his eyes for a moment. "What is it, Dawson?" he asked briskly. He let his glasses fall back down around his neck.

"I was thinking about everything you said. And you were right not to let me into your class."

Mr. Gold lifted a skeptical eyebrow. "I'm glad you gave it some thought."

"I did. However, I'm in a jam. I have a study hall fifth period in the library, and it's really crowded in there—major overflow, really sweaty and unpleasant—and I talked to Mr. Givens about switching study halls, and he seemed to think, with your permission, I could spend study halls with you."

"Fifth period? That's exactly when film class is," Mr. Gold said dryly.

"Now, that's an uncanny coincidence," Dawson said. He could do dry, too.

"You would not be part of the class," Mr. Gold continued. You'd sit in the back and be quiet. You wouldn't participate or involve yourself in any way."

"Thanks, Mr. Gold. I really mean that. This is a big deal."

She walked toward him.

"Morning . . . Miss Jacobs," Pacey said. Softly tailored black skirt, low-cut white blouse. She looked beautiful. Sexy. There was no getting away from it.

"Good morning, Pacey," she said tightly, eyes compelling him to go, not to start.

"Can we talk?"

"This isn't your class, Pacey. I'll see you later."

Uh-uh. She wasn't getting off the hook. "No." Pacey stood his ground. "We really need to talk."

Tamara put her books down on her desk and looked away from him. "We have nothing to discuss, Pacey, except homework of which there is none, so you can run along." He thought he heard a note of desperation in her voice. But she had made her own bed. Did she think she could play with his head and then expect him to just go away?

"There's a lot to discuss." He felt his anger from the other night returning. "We can start with the open-mouthed kiss if you'd like."

More students were coming in. People were looking at them. Tamara glanced at her class, then back to Pacey, pleadingly. "I don't know what you're talking about. I'm going to have to insist you leave this classroom immediately." She put on her voice of authority, but it just wasn't working.

Pacey actually felt a little sorry for her. "Listen." His voice softened. "I'm just as confused as you are." Wicked understatement. Anger, desire, desperation . . . fear. Pacey was a battleground.

"Pacey, please!" Tamara's voice sounded as if it might break. "Nothing happened. There was no . . . kiss." She dropped the word in a whisper. "Please. Don't." Pacey saw that her hands were shaking. Unshed tears formed in the corners of her hazel eyes.

The bell shattered the silence between them. Her students were in their seats.

Pacey dropped his voice to a whisper too. But his anger was strong. "Your tongue was in my mouth. You're not being fair." He turned his back to her abruptly and stormed toward the door.

"Good morning, everyone," he heard her saying, her voice wavering on the brink of control.

Powwow in the lunchroom. Dawson was a hundred percent earnest, a hundred percent focused. And here they all were again—Joey, Pacey, Jen, and Dawson. Hadn't they learned a thing from their little adventure at the Rialto? Joey wondered.

"I can't count on the film class for support, as I was hoping," Dawson explained. "It means we'll have to work overtime to meet the festival deadline. We'll have to shoot all weekend. And, Joey, that means no lip about giving Pacey lip."

Joey shot a glance at Pacey's bum eye. His little souvenir from the other night was turning a rainbow of nasty colors. Pacey hardly needed a mask to play a monster from the deep. "I'm reaching my breaking point with this whole kiss thing," she announced.

"I'm not engorged with this, either," Pacey told

her. "It goes both ways, you know." He bit into his hot dog.

Dawson blew out an exasperated breath.

Dawson looked at Joey, then at Jen. He looked torn. Then suddenly he smiled. "Joey, major revelation!"

Joey felt herself go tight. Not another semi-quasi double-date idea.

"Joey, I think I've figured out how to make you the happiest actress in the world."

Back to the film, Bob. Phew. Joey relaxed.

"You know how you die at the end of the movie? How would you like it if you died sooner? Like tomorrow?"

"What do you mean?" Like Dawson murders Joey on Friday. Goes to the dance with Jen on Saturday?

"Your character, in a surprise attack, is killed violently," Dawson told Joey, a little too enthusiastically. He spun toward Jen. "And your beautiful and bright cousin from New York arrives just in time to discover your mutilated body."

"Dude, you're on to something," Pacey said approvingly.

Joey felt a chill that was altogether too real. New girl's here—you're out, Joe.

But it was Jen who rallied to her side. "Whoa!" Jen protested. "Wait a minute."

"No, it's perfect," Dawson insisted. "Isn't it, Joey?" He was smiling at her expectantly. Had Dawson lost it? "It nullifies the kiss issue and gets you back behind the camera with me, where you belong."

Huh. Sometimes you just couldn't see the forest for the trees. Or something like that. Joey liked the way it sounded—back with Dawson, where she belonged. Plus, she'd gotten out of the most repellent kiss in town. No small deal.

But Jen was a few steps behind this time. "But haven't you already filmed a lot with Joey's character?"

"Easy cover," Dawson said. "It's better this way. It's so unpredictable. The audience will never see it coming. It's like Janet Leigh in *Psycho.*"

"Or Drew Barrymore in *Scream,*" Pacey put in.

"A rip-off of a rip-off," Joey said, nodding.

"I really think it fits right in line with the tone of the piece. Don't you see?" Dawson asked.

Joey saw. She saw herself and Dawson on one side of the camera. Jen and Pacey on . . . Hold everything. Jen and Pacey. The kiss. Jen was the new romantic lead. The kiss with Pacey was her responsibility now. Joey looked from Jen to Pacey. Or rather Pacey's hideous eye. She smiled. "You're right, Dawson. It's perfect."

# Chapter 12

Pacey was front and center, making sure Miss Jacobs felt his eyes on her every move. She wasn't getting off the hook so easily. He wasn't going to let her ignore him and pretend nothing had happened. Or that she'd played no role in that nothing.

The problem was that Pacey was supposed to be furious. He *was* furious. But he couldn't focus his rage on Tamara without looking at her and feeling something entirely different mixed in.

"Can someone explain to me the state of Catherine's mind as she drove Heathcliff away?" she was saying.

Pacey could barely concentrate on her words. As she studiously avoided looking at him, Pacey stared at the swell of her breasts under her white blouse, at her hips, at her perfect legs, her face, her lips. . . .

He tried to call up the sharpness of his anger, but he kept remembering how his lips had felt on her lips, the feel of her body pressed against his, the curve of her back under his hands. . . .

"Ooh, Miss Jacobs!" Nellie's voice brought him crashing back to planet high school. Hard to get romantic with Nellie's voice in his head.

"Yes? Ah, Nellie, is it?"

"The answer is that it was her tragic and dysfunctional way of letting him know she loved him," Nellie said dramatically.

"That's the obvious interpretation of the moment," Tamara said. She was straining with the effort to keep her eyes fixed on the back of the room. Pacey could see it. She was just as aware of him as he was of her. She couldn't hide from it. "However, I think it goes deeper than that. For some reason, this novel is regarded as a great love story," she went on. "But the reality is that Heathcliff and Catherine never should have been together."

Really? News to Emily Brontë, Pacey thought. Or was it Charlotte who'd written *Wuthering Heights*? One of those sisters. Definitely news to William Wyler and the 1939 movie version he'd directed with Merle Oberon and Laurence Olivier. Or Peter Kosminsky and his 1992 version starring Juliette Binoche and Ralph Fiennes. Pacey began to pay a little more attention to what Tamara was saying.

"They were all wrong for each other. Catherine was essentially a mess."

Pacey started getting a weird feeling.

"Heathcliff was basically a decent guy who had a

lot to learn about life and was inherently better off without some whimpering, mentally unstable wet rag following him around," Tamara said passionately. "The whole thing was wrong—never should have happened."

Oh, my God. Pacey was getting a command performance.

Tamara let her gaze wander to him for the briefest second. Then it snapped back to that most fascinating of fascinating back walls. "Emily Brontë should have saved her ink," she concluded.

Someone in the class gave a low whistle. People were looking at her as if maybe she'd lost it. But Pacey heard her loud and clear. What ever happened to letting your students make up their own minds, Miss Jacobs?

"Enter Stephanie's cousin," Dawson noted in his script as he started writing in the new role for Jen. Mr. Gold may have banished him to the back of the room and sentenced him to silence, but this was fifth-period film class, and he was going to work on his film like everyone else.

Up at the front, Mr. Gold was addressing a tall, muscular boy with thick, dark hair and the chiseled face of a Greek sculpture. "We'll have to move fast if we're going to enter the film festival," the teacher was saying to him.

The film festival? Dawson put down his script.

"We can make it," Mr. Perfect was saying. "The script is done. The movie's boarded. We did a lot of the work over the summer." Dawson felt a tug of anguish. Wouldn't you know it? Gold's special student. The guy was a couple of grades ahead of him, but Dawson knew who he was. Everyone did. Cliff Elliot, a.k.a. Mr. Perfect, was the Capeside Wildcats quarterback—picture in the paper all the time, already being wooed by the college scouts. And if that wasn't enough, he was student council chairman, an A student, and the secret dream of more than a few Capeside girls. That stock character in every teen drama. You had to hate the guy on principle alone.

"I'll need a finalized budget before I can greenlight any shooting," Mr. Gold said to him.

Cliff turned to Nellie, sitting by his side. "The figures haven't changed," she said, giving Cliff a gooey smile. "We're still under budget."

Under budget. Dawson snorted to himself. Only Cliff. What film in the history of films had ever come in under budget? But even Mr. Gold was under the guy's spell.

"Then let's move to the story," the teacher said. Did you solve your third-act problem?"

Dawson couldn't believe this. Cliff Perfect's movie was going to the film festival. His would be the one official entry from Capeside High. Week one, and it was already decided. Dawson shot his hand up, waved it vigorously.

Mr. Gold lifted his glasses to his eyes and looked at him. "Yes, Dawson," he said, his voice heavy with indulgence.

"Would that be the Boston Film Festival?" Dawson asked.

"Yes, that's correct. They sponsor a junior-level video competition."

*My* film festival. Cliff's film is going to *my* film festival. Dawson got a sinking feeling as Cliff stood and addressed the class.

"Okay, I've just been injured in the big game with Tyler. My throwing arm has been crushed, the bone broken in three places. But I refuse to tell the coach because he won't let me play at homecoming if I do."

Dawson had heard this somewhere before.

"Remember," Cliff said, "we want the audience asking, 'Can he do it?' 'Will the team win the big game?'"

Correction. He'd heard this everywhere before— every B-rated sports flick that had ever been made.

"Remember, this is autobiographical, so if anybody has any questions, I was there, I lived it. Come talk to me, all right?" Cliff was saying.

Of course. Capeside's final game last year. Dawson made it a habit not to read the local sports section of the paper: "Mrs. Mason's Grandson Bats Fly Ball through Neighbor's Window." But even Dawson hadn't managed to miss this story. He'd even seen his mother report it on TV: Capeside victory, starring Cliff Perfect.

And now Cliff was going to replay it. In living color. At Dawson's festival. With Ben Gold's blessing.

Cute, Jen thought. More than cute, actually. The guy looked kind of like a living version of a Greek sculpture. Wonder what he looks like with just his fig leaf?

The guy must have felt her gaze. He shut his locker and looked over at her. Jen smiled. He smiled. And came over to her.

"Hi, I'm Cliff."

Oh. So he was the one. Nellie had mentioned him when she cornered Jen on the front steps of school a few mornings ago. No lie about the way he looked.

"Hi, I'm Jen."

"Short for Jennifer. I know. You're new."

"Is it that obvious? I was hoping to blend in," Jen joked.

"Sorry, but that's an impossibility on your part," Cliff tossed back flirtatiously.

Jen laughed. "I'll work on it."

"Well, I just wanted to introduce myself. I know that being the new kid can be traumatic, and if there's anything I can do to take the edge off, like show you around, introduce you to some cool people, take you out, maybe to dinner and a movie . . ."

"Subtle," Jen commented. The guy moved fast.

"It was meant to be assertive," Cliff said lightly.

"That's very nice of you." Jen had to admit she was enjoying the attention. But she'd left "fast" in New York. "Can I let you know? It's the first week. I'm still getting settled."

"Sure," Cliff said easily enough. "Absolutely, and I meant what I said about helping out. I know a lot of people around here. I can hook you up with some friends."

Cliff smiled.

"It was nice to meet you, Jen—short for Jennifer."

"You too, Cliff—short for Clifford."

# Chapter 13

$D$awson grabbed the latex version of Joey's head off his desk. "Morning, Joe," he said to the mask.

He bounded down the stairs and into the living room. His father was already up, huddled over his restaurant model, playing dollhouse. "Have you seen my camcorder, Dad?"

His father looked up. "You filming, today?"

Dawson held up Joey's rubber head. "Joey gets decapitated."

"Cool," Mitch Leery said. "Your camera's in my room. On the nightstand—your mother's side."

Dawson headed back up the stairs toward his parents' bedroom.

His father's voice followed him: "But you might want to take the tape out."

Dawson froze in midstep. Well, thank you for

sharing that with me, Dad. "You know, you can get arrested for that in some states," he said.

His father just grinned and went back to playing with his model.

"Um, Dad? While we're on the subject of . . . well . . ."

His father looked right at him. Full attention this time.

"I have a question. It's a girl-slash-relationship question," Dawson plunged in. He hadn't really meant to talk to his dad about this, but he hadn't really meant for his dad to bring the whole thing up, either. "I don't want it to go to your head like I'm soliciting fatherly advice or anything," he added quickly.

"What's the question?" his father asked.

"Because I clearly don't condone your perverse sex life—yours and Mom's—but I'm not too proud to admit that my inexperience is hindering my current female relations. . . ."

"And the question?" his father repeated, breaking into Dawson's rambling monologue.

Dawson shifted uncomfortably. He shouldn't have brought this up. His dad shouldn't have brought it up. "The question . . . The subject, actually." But he might as well finish what he'd started. "Mechanics of kissing."

His dad didn't try too hard to conceal a smile. "How can I help?"

"I'm interested in technique."

Mr. Leery laughed. "There is no technique, Dawson. You just put your lips together and go."

A no-answer answer. "But what makes a good kiss?" Dawson persevered.

"Performance anxiety?" his father asked.

Well, Dawson hadn't gotten to the performance yet. Only the rehearsal. In his head. Which was part of the problem. In his head, the kiss was climactic. Bogart. Brando. Leonardo DiCaprio. And what about the kiss in Jen's head? The one she'd said she was going to pretend had happened. What if it was equally awesome? And what if the performance didn't match up to the rehearsal? "I'm just a little confused about what distinguishes a good kiss from a superior kiss," he admitted.

"You'll know. In a big way," Mitch Leery added, passionately but vaguely.

"Could you expound?"

"You have to make it memorable. Something she can't forget."

Details, Dad. It's nothing without the details. "And how would you do that?" Dawson prodded.

"The first time I kissed your mother—"

"Don't get too detailed," Dawson interrupted. There were details and there were details.

"It was summer, and we were out on the boat," Mitch Leery continued. "And your mother's lips were chapped from the sun, and she asked to borrow my Chap Stick, so I took it out and put some on my lips, and then I leaned over and kissed her."

Okay. Dawson could see it. Well, with some other actors playing Mom's and Dad's roles.

"The Chap Stick was really smooth and just slid onto her lips. The sensation was amazing. The chemistry between us was already there, but it was one of those moments that cemented it. You know. It was unforgettable and, most important, romantic."

Dawson was surprised. "And here I thought you were all about sex."

"We still jumped each other. But you gotta have romance. It's all about romance . . . and Chap Stick," Mr. Leery added.

All right, good story. But what had Dawson learned? Besides row softly and carry a big Chap Stick? "But the kiss itself. What did you do?"

Mitch Leery thought for a moment. "Here's how it works. You clear your mind. Just think about her lips—nothing else."

Okay. Easy enough. Dawson had gotten that far already.

"Don't tense up. That destroys a kiss. And you gotta relax. Here . . ." Suddenly Dawson's dad grabbed the latex model of Joey's head. He held it up so that Dawson was staring her in the face. "Give it a try."

What! "Forget it," Dawson said. He backed away from the head.

His father stretched it out toward him. "C'mon. This is a big father-son moment. You asked for it."

No. His father had started it. With the camcorder. Of course, Dawson had asked for it. He wanted to know. Needed to know. He looked at Joey's head. This was too weird. Her lips. "Just think about her lips—nothing else," his dad had said. Dawson looked at the lips. Okay, they were nice lips. He'd told Joey that himself.

"Now, moisten your lips," his father was instructing.

Dawson followed instructions. The lips. Nothing but the lips . . .

"Now go for it. The trick is to relax your bottom lip. You want to let it have a mind of its own. You want it to dance with hers." His father moved the head into position.

The lips. Her lips. Dawson pressed his lips against Joey's.

Joey couldn't believe she was seeing this. She couldn't believe she was watching Dawson kiss her. Up at the top of the stairs, she peered through the railing, like a little girl spying on the grown-ups downstairs.

She'd come in the usual way—up the ladder and into Dawson's room—but she'd heard his voice downstairs. She hadn't meant to spy. She'd been on her way down when she saw them. Saw them and froze, incredulous. Mr. Leery was giving a kissing lesson to Dawson, using her head.

Now she studied Dawson as he pressed his mouth to the mask. Dawson was kissing her! She pictured herself—her real self—down there instead. His lips on her lips—yes, dancing, warm, moist. . . .

"Close your eyes," Mr. Leery was saying.

Joey let her eyes close. Dawson's arms around her, their mouths searching, tentative, then deeper, with intensity. . . .

"That's it," Dawson's father said.

Joey's eyes flew open. Dawson and his dad were

97

smiling at each other—Dawson sheepishly, his dad simply, proudly. A bonding moment. Between father and son. Not between her and Dawson. Joey gave her head a hard shake.

"That was good," Mr. Leery was saying downstairs.

"Yeah? Cool," Dawson responded. "Now forget this ever happened." He grabbed the Joey head roughly and headed toward the back door.

Joey felt a little shaky as she got to her feet. Best to go back down the ladder and forget she was ever here. Like she could really forget watching Dawson kiss that rubber mask with her face on it.

She backtracked to his room. But before she went through his door, she heard a giggle. She looked around. No one. But there it was again. A giggle and a whisper—coming from the hall closet. And then Joey saw the telephone cord snaking from the hall extension under the closet door.

"Okay, I promise," said the voice. The voice of the local news. The voice of Mrs. Leery. "Bye."

The closet door flew open. Dawson's mother, phone in hand, stifled a little shriek. "Joey! What are you doing here?"

"I was looking for Dawson. We're filming today," Joey explained. And what are you doing? she wanted to ask. Mrs. Leery's face was flushed. She definitely looked as if she'd been caught in the act. Whatever act it was.

"Filming?" Mrs. Leery echoed, flustered. "That's nice."

"I get killed today," Joey said.

"That's nice," Mrs. Leery repeated.

Guilty. Absolutely guilty. Joey faced Dawson's mother. Back to you, Bob. My God, Dawson was right.

Mrs. Leery shut the closet door and put the telephone on the little table in the hall. She turned back to Joey. "Secret anniversary present for Mitch," she said. "I'm making plans, and I don't want him to hear. Twenty years, it'll be."

Yeah?

"Don't say anything."

"Of course not," Joey said.

"Twenty years," Mrs. Leery repeated. "First time he kissed me was in a little rowboat." She got a faraway look in her eyes. "Like the one you use to come over here."

Joey was suddenly irritated with herself. What kind of script was she writing here? Twenty years was a long time, and Mr. and Mrs. Leery were still all over each other.

"Well, be careful out in the sun," Mrs. Leery said. "It's hot today. Use sunblock."

"Thanks, Mrs. Leery. See ya," Joey said.

"You too, Joey."

Joey turned to leave. This was Dawson's fault. His film fantasy conflict bug was catching. As if life didn't present enough conflicts. Like seeing your best friend kiss a rubber model of your face.

# Chapter 14

**J**oey moved down the dock toward her rowboat. The sun was shining. The water was calm. A few birds chirped cheerfully. But you could see that something was wrong.

"Steven? Steven?" she called out.

Her glance fell on something lying at the edge of the dock. A towel? A piece of clothing? She walked over for a closer look. Leaned down toward it. A shirt. She began to pick it up.

"Aah!" She sucked her breath in, fear on her face. The shirt was torn and splattered with blood. "Steven!" her voice rang out, panicked.

She peered into the water. Suddenly the sea creature was upon her. Somehow more real, more nasty-looking than last time. She screamed, lashing out at the creature and bashing it on the head.

The creature fell away back into the water. Joey raced back up the dock, but the creature was pulling himself up on one of the solid wood piles. He clawed his way out of the water, and rose up to his full height on the dock, blocking her way back to the creek bank.

She spun around and ran for the other end of the dock. The creature lumbered after her. She jumped into her rowboat, grabbed the oars, and started to make a getaway, but the creature took a flying dive and landed in the water right next to the boat.

She screamed, struggling with the oars, but the creature latched on to the side of the rowboat with one taloned green claw. With the other one, he slashed at her face. Tore a raw, dripping wound right down her cheek.

Joey screamed bloody murder. The creature slashed his talons across her neck. Her head fell back as he sliced her neck open. Blood sprayed into the air like a geyser. He slashed again. Her head went flying off. More blood sprayed into the blue sky.

Joey's head fell into the bottom of the boat. Her body slumped nearby.

Dawson focused the camera in on the head, lying in a rich pool of blood. The head he'd kissed this morning . . . Uh-uh. He wasn't going there. "And . . . cut! Beautiful. Perfect."

At his side, Jen began to applaud. The real Joey stood up and emerged from the mess in the boat. She was covered, head to toe, with fake blood.

"That couldn't have gone better," Dawson said as she climbed onto the dock.

Pacey came onto shore, too, stripping off his creature costume. "Joey, you die so well," he said. "Dawson, can we do it again? Please? I so liked the image."

"No. Moving on," Dawson said, leaving no room for discussion. "We're behind schedule."

He saw Joey flash Pacey a victorious smile.

Joey was dripping fake blood all over Dawson's front porch. Jen carried out a bowl of soapy water and a towel from the kitchen. She put the bowl down on the porch table and dipped the edge of the towel in it.

"Here, Joey. Let me help you," she said.

Joey shied away. "It's okay. I can do it."

"I don't mind." Jen approached with the towel.

Joey felt a wave of discomfort. She didn't need a cleanup crew. She tugged at her button-front blouse. Ugh. The fake blood had started to dry in the sun, and her shirt stuck to her skin as if the blood were real.

"Ouch," Jen said sympathetically. "Looks like it's really stuck on you."

Before Joey could stop her, Jen took hold of the open neck of the shirt and gently pried it away from Joey's body. She reached for the top button and started to undo it.

Joey felt every muscle in her body clench up. What did Jen think she was doing? She looked into Jen's face, just inches from her own. Met her gaze.

Jen's hands went still, immobilized on Joey's blouse. Joey began to protest, then stopped. Was she being squeamish? Uptight? Jen was just going for the Miss Friendship Award, right? Like she'd been trying to do since she came on the scene.

Jen gingerly undid Joey's top button and wiped at her neckline with the towel. Carefully. Softly. Joey's discomfort swelled. Jen went for the next button down.

Joey abruptly pulled away. "I can do it," she said. She felt her cheeks grow pink. Turning slightly away from Jen, she unbuttoned her shirt and peeled it off her skin. Jen took the shirt from her and handed her the towel. Hot with self-consciousness, Joey began cleaning herself off.

"You have nice breasts," Jen said.

Joey froze. Deer in headlights. Well, Joey's headlights. Jen's eyes on them.

"Don't get the wrong idea," Jen said quickly. "I'm completely hetero. I'm just commenting girl to girl. You have a really nice body."

Joey rapidly finished cleaning herself up and pulled on a clean T-shirt she had set out on the porch rocker earlier. Just girl talk? Jen sounded sincere. She was just so unflappably friendly to Joey. Why? If Joey was nasty, Jen was nice. If Joey was nice, Jen was nice. Not bimbo nice, though. The girl had wit. Sharp wit. Joey was sure she could be nasty if she chose to.

It was too hard to figure out a strategy. "I'm too tall," Joey said, resorting to what she really felt.

Jen shook her head. "No, you're not at all . . . you're commanding."

She was? Joey was silent.

"I wish I had your stature," Jen said.

Uh-oh, thought Joey. She'd let a little honesty in, and now they were playing True Confessions. Best buds suddenly.

"And your long legs," Jen continued. "My body's a mess. I'm short. My hips do this weird thing, my face is shaped like a duck's, and I hate my breasts."

Despite herself, Joey felt empathy—and astonishment. "Are you serious?" Jen had to know how beautiful she was. That when she'd come down the dock that first day, Dawson and Pacey had been stupid with awe.

Jen shrugged. "It's normal, isn't it? To hate the way you look?"

Well, maybe Joey wouldn't have minded looking a little more like Bess—even though people told her there was a strong family resemblance—or a little more like, well . . . someone like Jen.

"You don't look like a duck."

Jen looked at her for a long moment. And smiled. "You know, that's the nicest thing you've said to me since we met." She grabbed the dirty towel and shirt and headed for the door. "I'm going to take these in and clean them up."

Joey felt a breath of relief. Enough of all this sweetness. She licked a streak of fake blood off her finger. She couldn't handle much more of this.

But Jen had one last remark as she went through

the door. "Joey? I plan to make it really hard for you not to like me," she said.

The sun was dropping quickly. Perfect. The darkening sky was just the right effect. Jen and Pacey stood at the end of the dock, talking. The creek glinted in the last light of the day. Dawson trained his camera on the spot where Joey had been decapitated, then focused in on Jen and Pacey.

"Don't worry," Pacey said. "I'll help you find your cousin."

"That's very sweet of you," Jen replied. Close-up on her, on the softness of her face. God, she was pretty. Then back just far enough for a full-body shot. Dawson let the camera follow the lines of her figure, caress them. Back a little more to see her and Pacey together.

"I can't thank you enough," she said with a smile. She looked into Pacey's eyes gratefully. Then she leaned closer to him and kissed him gently, simply.

In an instant Pacey's arms were around her, and he was going in for something more. His mouth pressed down. His lips were . . . dancing. Dawson experienced a moment of paralyzed shock. The kiss kept going. The camera kept capturing it.

"Cut!" Dawson yelled. "Pacey, what are you doing?"

Jen and Pacey broke apart. Dawson stormed over. Pacey's hand still rested on Jen's shoulder.

"What?" Pacey was an innocent. "I'm kissing. What does it look like I'm doing?"

"Snorkeling." Dawson gave Pacey a shove,

knocking his hand away from Jen. "And that's not the way it's scripted."

Jen gave a breezy laugh. Dawson looked at her. The laugh settled into a little smile. She didn't seem too much the worse for wear.

Behind him, Dawson heard Joey laughing too. She came down the dock to join the little party. "It was just a kiss, Dawson." Damn Joey. She was loving this.

"Yeah, and you know what? Honestly, I think we should have another," Pacey suggested.

"No." Dawson spun on Pacey. "I'm cutting the kiss. No kiss."

"Whoa. Wait a second," Joey protested. "You can't cut the kiss."

Dawson took a deep breath. Spielberg, he told himself. "Yes, I can," he said, regaining his composure. "And I just did. It's not working. It doesn't make sense for this new character to kiss her dead cousin's boyfriend. The kiss is officially cut."

Pacey shrugged and started walking up the dock. "Then that means it's a wrap, right? 'Cause I've got plans tonight."

Dawson had had enough of Pacey's hot plans already. "Yeah, that's a wrap. Get outta here."

Joey watched Dawson follow Jen across the lawn toward her grandparents' house. Back near the dock, Joey began packing up the camera equipment. Well, that had been fun, but as they said, all good things must come to an end. And there was Dawson tagging after Jen like a faithful puppy. And here she was, watching Pacey of the Rainbow Eye as he stripped out of his creeped-up wet suit, revealing only the skimpy bathing trunks he'd worn under his costume.

"And what are you up to this evening?" she asked with only mild curiosity.

"It just so happens that the woman of my dreams is attending the school dance tonight, and I plan on being there," Pacey said.

"Lucky her," Joey commented. She wasn't really that interested in who it was, but she did wonder if the woman of his dreams kissed as well as Jen.

Dawson and Jen walked toward her grandparents' house. He was fully aware that they were tracing the route to their pretend kiss, but he tried to keep things easier this time.

"So in honor of the school dance, I rented *Saturday Night Fever, Staying Alive,* and *Grease,*" he said.

Jen looked at him questioningly. "In lieu of going?"

"Yeah, it'll be a John Travolta night of interpretive expression. This way we can dance, and our feet never have to move." He laughed. But he noticed Jen wasn't laughing along.

"I can't, Dawson." She looked away from him. "I'm sorry."

Dawson felt a punch of disappointment. But he tried not to let it show. "More enticing plans?" he asked.

"Actually, I'm going to go to the dance, Dawson."

To the dance? As in school spirit? As in "Rah-rah, Capeside"?

"I'm sorry. I didn't know you wanted to do the movie thing," she explained.

"Oh." Well, he hadn't told her. His fault. "That's okay," he said, unconvincingly. "You . . . going alone?"

Jen was quiet. Very quiet for a moment. Dawson felt a grip of dread. "No. Actually, Cliff Elliot asked me."

Dawson felt himself clench up inside. This was even worse than he'd expected.

"He thought it would be a good opportunity for me to meet some people," Jen went on hurriedly. As if her explanation made it all okay.

"Oh." Dawson didn't know what to say.

"C'mon, Dawson. Don't look so down. It's not like a date or anything. He just asked me if I wanted to go, and I said yes."

Dawson felt his defeat take on a bitter edge. "Call me confused. That's the definition of a date, Jen."

Jen looked right at him. Studied his face. "Yeah, you're right," she said softly. "I just wanted to go, you know. I'm new here in Capeside, and it sounded fun."

Dawson thought back to the other day in the lunchroom. Nellie inviting them all to the dance. Yeah, Jen had said she thought it sounded great. Okay, so Dawson didn't usually do dances, but why hadn't he listened a little harder?

"Hey," Jen said brightly, "why don't you show

up? We could dance," she said with a smile. A real smile. Dawson could see she meant it.

But what about Cliff Perfect? Cliff had asked Jen out. Jen had said yes. Was Dawson supposed to show up and hang with both of them? Maybe have a few dozen chances to hear about Cliff playing the homecoming game with his arm broken in three places?

"Nah, I've got a date with Travolta," Dawson said, way more casually than he felt. "I don't want to disappoint him."

"Yeah. Okay," Jen said guardedly. "See ya, Dawson."

She went inside. Dawson wandered back across to his house. He was miserable. Pure, unadulterated misery. What had happened to "I'm going to pretend we kissed, Dawson"?

He kind of wished some hideous sea creature would come up out of the depths and put him out of his misery.

*Chapter 15*

Dawson was out of his mind. Ranting, shell-shocked, a character in one of his own scripts. Joey stretched out in the middle of Dawson's bed and watched him pace back and forth. Window to wall, wall to window, again and again. It was a little like following a Ping-Pong match.

"Cliff!" Dawson spewed. "Cliff Elliot. What is *that* about? I don't get it. How could she be attracted to him? What's he got?"

"You could start with his chest measurement and work down," Joey suggested. Jen did seem to have a good eye.

"No, beyond the external," Dawson said, so worked up he answered her seriously. "There's nothing going on in here." He pointed to his head. "Head fumes. That's it. The guy's a lightweight.

You know what his film is called? You wanna know?"

"What's his film called, Dawson?"

"*Helmets of Glory.* It chronicles last year's football season. And get this—Mr. Cliff Perfect himself is writing, directing, and starring in it."

"A real Streisand," Joey commented.

Dawson stopped pacing just long enough to frown at her. "This is serious, Joey. Listen, that's this year's Capeside High entry in the film festival. *My* film festival."

"And it's a sports film," Joey egged him on.

"A thin and pedestrian sports film," Dawson concurred.

"The epitome of everything you're against. Could life be more cruel?"

"You're laughing at me, Joe. The point is that his script is ludicrous and his story sense is even worse." Dawson pounded his hand on the TV, as if *Helmets of Glory* might have made it to the small screen right in front of their eyes. "And this is my immediate competition."

"In more ways than one," Joey noted. "Dawson, I don't think his cinematic prowess is the attraction."

Dawson kept rolling, like a video that kept playing long after its viewer had fallen asleep in the armchair. "What kills me is she was so open about it. 'I'm going with Cliff Elliot.' Like it wouldn't bother me. I respect her candor, but it's a little on the thoughtless side, you know."

"Completely thoughtless," Joey echoed automatically. Where was the Stop button?

"At this very moment they're slow dancing. Her arms are wrapped around his waist and they're moving to some stupid, cheesy eighties song."

Well, Dawson was nothing if not good at setting the scene for his stories. Joey heard 'Eternal Flame' start to play in her head. Saw all those couples out on the dance floor, felt her interest starting to spark again.

"And he's whispering things in her ear that make her giggle and throw her hair to one side, and every once in a while their eyes meet and they shift awkwardly and uncomfortably because they both know that it's all leading to that one moment at night's end when he leans over and tells her what a great time he had."

Okay. Joey could see it. Teen love. Party of two.

"He asks if they can do it again, and she just smiles in that sexy, teasing way that doesn't seem teasing at all—just sexy—and she says, 'I'd like that,' and then their lips meet, their mouths come together, their tongues find each other . . . Aaahhh! I can't take it!"

Dawson flung himself onto the bed and collapsed next to Joey. The soliloquy was over.

"You are so dramatic," Joey said.

Dawson rolled over on his side and looked at her. "What did he do that I didn't?"

Joey was incredulous. "He. Asked. Her. Out," she said, measuring the space between words for the extra emphasis Dawson sorely needed.

Dawson's eyes opened wider. Joey could see the light of recognition pop on. This was a new and mind-bending thought to him. Joey couldn't believe it. Their voices dropped, they got a little body hair—and something happened to their brains.

Suddenly Dawson was leaping off the bed. "I'm going to the dance," he announced with determination.

"What!" Dawson didn't do dances. Dawson had never been to a dance in his life.

"I'm going. It's my only recourse."

"Why?" John Travolta was still waiting for them.

Dawson yanked open his closet and began searching the rack for something. "Because Jen is there," he answered.

"In the arms of another man," Joey reminded him. "Why torture yourself?"

Dawson pulled a blue, button-down shirt off a hanger and started changing. "I'm an artist. 'Tortured' is a prerequisite. Are you coming, or not?"

Joey wasn't very happy about giving up their triple feature. They hadn't hung out and watched movies all night since Jen had arrived. And besides, beneath the glib words she and Dawson liked to toss back and forth, she was actually worried about him. "Think it through, Dawson. This little movie plot you've got going may not end the way you want it to."

She was mad at Dawson. Okay, she had to admit it. Not to anyone else and certainly not to him, but she didn't like sharing him with Jen. Still, she didn't want to see Jen break his heart, either.

But Dawson was already playing the romantic lead. "I should be the one kissing her, Joey. Not some J. Crew ad. I can make my bottom lip dance. I know it!"

Joey had a flash of their kiss—Dawson and hers, or rather her head's. He'd been working that dancing lip just the way his father had told him to. At least in her mind.

"Tonight it will happen," Dawson decreed. "This plot will have a happy ending, Joey. You'll see. Tonight I'm going to kiss the girl."

And he didn't mean a latex mask, either. Joey sighed and got to her feet. She couldn't get into watching all those videos alone and having to imagine what was going on at the dance. Better to see it live. To face the pitiful truth.

"This is so pathetic, Dawson. But I am not above witnessing your hormonal suicide. Count me in."

Dawson smiled for the first time all night. Not the happiest smile, but it was something. "I'll meet you downstairs. Give me two seconds. Let me check my hair."

He raced into the bathroom as Joey made her way to the stairs. She pulled on her sweater, and halfway down the stairs she stopped to tie one sneaker. Mrs. Leery's voice floated up the stairs.

"We probably won't discuss the telethon until after dinner, so it could be late."

Joey glanced down. Dawson's mother was leaning over his father. She lowered her mouth onto his. "Mmm . . ." They kissed. And kissed. And kissed.

Finally Mrs. Leery broke away. "I'll shoot for midnight," she told her husband.

Joey was almost out of breath just watching that

kiss. Man, Mr. and Mrs. Leery were lucky. Joey thought about her own parents. The way her dad had run around on her mom forever. And how it had torn her mom apart. Destroyed her. Literally. The cancer came on the heels of her father's most sordid little fling. No matter how you did the math, he had put her six feet under.

Joey swallowed back the lump in her throat. She didn't want to think about it. She wasn't going to think about it. She just wished Dawson would understand how lucky he was. His parents had everything. And he had everything too. So why shouldn't he get the girl?

"Ready?" He came down the stairs behind her.

Joey turned and looked up at him.

"Joe? You okay?"

"Yeah. Sure," Joey said. "Dawson?"

"Uh-huh?"

"You know, I was thinking maybe your movie *will* have a happy ending."

*Chapter 16*

Jen and Cliff sipped aqua-blue drinks with little plastic fish floating around in them. The gym looked like the inside of an aquarium, nets and huge pieces of papier-mâché coral everywhere, sea life painted on the walls and hanging from the ceiling like mobiles. Vintage Beach Boys was a favorite with the DJ—in between Madonna and the Bangles' "Eternal Flame." The dance floor was crowded with kids.

"Fortunately, this is a victory dance," Cliff said over the music.

Jen took a sip of her blue punch. "And did you make the winning play?"

Cliff smiled at her. The Greek-sculpture smile. "You're here, aren't you?" he said smoothly.

Jen smiled back. "That could have been my exit cue, but somehow you pulled it off." She liked Cliff.

More than she'd expected to. He wasn't Dawson. But Dawson wasn't here, was he? And then there was Joey. It was probably better this way. Cliff was easy to be with. And certainly easy on the eyes.

"I sold it?" Cliff asked lightly.

"Oh, yes. You're smooth yet unassuming. It's endearing," Jen teased back. "Is there anything you're not good at?"

"Dancing," Cliff admitted. "I'm rhythmically challenged."

Jen hoped he was being modest. She loved to dance. "Prove it," she said.

Cliff nodded. He took their drinks and set them down on a nearby table. Then he led her onto the dance floor.

Pacey nodded to the girls he passed. Smiled. Cool. Suave. Bond. James Bond. The strawberry blonde over there looked good in her little black dress. Cute friend in forest-green velvet. Shaken, not stirred, ladies.

All of a sudden he spotted her. And the game was over. Tamara. Over by the punch bowl with that Benji guy—revealed on that humiliating night at the movies as Ben Gold, Dawson's film teacher. Cool melted into nervous and hot. Suave into unsteady.

Mr. Gold moved away, and Tamara was left standing by herself. Pacey felt even more uncertain. Now what? She was wearing a simple midnight-blue dress, nothing as revealing as what she'd had on that first time in the video store, but she looked incredibly sexy. Incredibly desirable. And Pacey knew what it felt like to hold her in his arms. To taste her lips.

He walked over. "Evening . . . Miss Jacobs."

She smiled awkwardly. "Hello, Pacey. How are you this evening?"

"Confused," Pacey answered honestly. "Bewildered. Perplexed. Mystified. A thesaurus of emotion."

The corners of Tamara's mouth turned down. "You know, I'm the chaperon, Pacey. I should make the rounds." She took one step.

Pacey moved in front of her. Close to her. Close enough to feel the electricity between them. "Would you like to dance, Tamara?" he asked softly.

He could see that she was as torn apart as he was. Her hazel eyes gleamed with pent-up emotion. She let her gaze drop. "That's not a good idea, Pacey."

"Of course it's not a good idea. But if things were different, would you?"

"I have to go," Tamara whispered. She side-stepped him and took off across the gym.

"Prepare to descend, Captain," Dawson said uneasily as he checked out the gym and the aquarium decor. Kinda like a full-scale version of his dad's restaurant. A cool band was pumping out their alterna-pop latest, and people were going wild on the dance floor. Go, Capeside.

He and Joey moved to the edge of the dance floor. Dawson scanned the room. It didn't take very long to spot her. Short black crocheted dress, baby T, bare legs, and black platform sandals. Or to spot him. To spot them.

Dawson watched Jen and Cliff moving to the beat. Cliff did a rolling wave kind of thing with his arms. Jen borrowed the gesture and turned it into something new. Cliff took the new movement and riffed on that. They were good.

"They make such a cute couple," Joey offered.

"Shut up," Dawson said.

"What exactly is your plan?"

Dawson felt a rush of desperation. "I didn't get that far."

"Well, you'd better write something quick," Joey said. "Because in some moral sectors what they're doing is known as foreplay."

Dawson grimaced. He was supposed to step into center stage now. But how? Jen and Cliff were swept up in their happy, shining world. The world that did school dances. The world that played football. The world that fit in. He was losing ground every second he stood here. He looked at Joey.

"Do you dance?" He knew the answer.

"Never."

"Now you do," Dawson corrected her. He grabbed her arm and pulled her onto the dance floor.

"Dawson, this is certifiable!" she protested.

"It'll be okay. Just jump around and shake your butt back and forth," Dawson said, as much to himself as to Joey.

He led her into the mass of writhing bodies, toward where Cliff and Jen were dancing. He let go of her arm and faced her, shifting tentatively from one foot to the other and nodding his head to the music. Joey shot him a skeptical look and worked her hands in a modified swimming motion.

And then it was over before it had started. The last notes of the song stretched out into a final chord. The lights in the gym dimmed even further, and the sound of softly lapping surf floated out of the loudspeakers, followed by the gentle, bluesy guitar notes of a slow song. Some of the dancers took it as a cue to move off the floor. The rest moved closer together, ready to glide silkenly and romantically to the music.

Dawson felt a ripple of panic. He looked at Joey. She looked at him. Advance or retreat? Dawson took Joey in his arms, simultaneously looking around for Jen.

"We lost her," he said in Joey's ear.

"Maybe she's with your brain," Joey retorted. But she put her arms around him.

It was surprisingly natural to start swaying to the tune. Dawson was dimly aware that this wasn't too unpleasant, even as he searched for Jen. He spun Joey around so he could get a glimpse of the other side of the room. Joey followed his lead, smoothly, gracefully. Dawson felt a little rush.

"Hey, you're pretty good at this," he whispered.

Joey didn't have an answer handy. But it was okay, because they filled in the wordlessness with the movement of their bodies to the music. Dawson felt himself relax into it. Not unpleasant at all.

"Hey, you guys." That caffeine feeling came rushing back at the sound of Jen's voice.

He and Joey turned in sync, to see Jen and Cliff right beside them. Twirling together as one.

"Hi," Dawson said cautiously.

"You made it," Jen noted brightly.

"Yeah."

"Guys, do you know Cliff?"

"Hi," Joey said. Dawson saw her start at the chest measurement and work down. Dawson gave Cliff a little nod.

"We have film class together, right?" Cliff asked him, easily spinning himself and Jen, so he and Dawson could hear each other.

"Not exactly. It's my study hall base."

"But Dawson is a very talented filmmaker," Jen put in quickly. Dawson would have appreciated it more if she hadn't been dancing in Cliff's arms.

"Oh, yeah?" Cliff asked. "You into movies?"

This was not going the way it was supposed to. The last thing Dawson had come here for was to have a cozy chat about film with Mr. *Helmets of Glory.* "I dabble," Dawson said dismissively.

"Cool," Cliff said.

Dawson felt his frustration building. Sometimes you had to know when to yell "cut."

"See ya," he said to Cliff and Jen. He spun Joey around and moved away. By the time the music ended Jen and Cliff were lost again.

Dawson and Joey let go of each other. "That went brilliantly," Joey said as they moved off the dance floor.

\* \* \*

From the sidelines, Pacey watched Tamara studiously watching the dancers. Eyes straight ahead, determined, diligent, intent. Totally focused on avoiding his gaze. She knew he was looking at her. Knew exactly where he was standing.

Pacey dropped his gaze, disgusted, beaten. Tamara knew he was hers for the asking, and she wasn't asking. Then there was the other approach. Make her think about what she was missing. Pacey frowned. A tired plot device, for sure. Especially when she was missing exactly nothing. It wasn't like he was seeing much action these days. Okay, any days, to be honest. But he was desperate. Desperate enough to grab Nellie when he saw her walking by.

"Hi, Nellie." Smile, he coached himself.

"Uh-huh," Nellie said distrustfully.

"Nice dance. I really like what you've done with the place."

Nellie gave him a hard look. "You almost seem pleasant, Pacey. Have you been drinking?"

Pacey glanced over at Tamara. Yes indeed. She was unmistakably watching him talk to Nellie. The smile he bestowed on Nellie grew all the more genuine.

"Drinking? No, not at all. I was just noticing the detail in your neon tetras."

"Your compliments are suspect."

"There's no ulterior motive here." Pacey did his best Boy Scout. "It's just that all this glorious underwater sea life has put my contempt for you in perspective, and I thought maybe you would like to . . . I don't know . . . dance with me . . . maybe." Shy.

Uncertain. Way to go. And Tamara was absolutely checking them out.

"That's very sweet of you," Nellie said. "To ask me. Me. Of all mankind."

Pacey took a step toward her, ready to lead her onto the dance floor. He could stomach it for Tamara's sake.

"Me, who really wouldn't mind if you dropped, on the spot, dead—right at this moment. And I wish I could take this moment to laugh in your face, but I'm getting slightly nauseated just standing next to you, so excuse me." Nellie wriggled the fingers of one hand in an overdone ta-ta. Then she was off.

Pacey quickly looked over at Tamara. But Tamara was chatting away with a couple of her students. She wasn't looking Pacey's way at all. So much for the other approach.

# Chapter 17

"Hey!" Dawson caught up with Jen in the hallway, where the music and voices from the gym were muted.

Jen whirled around, surprise showing on her face. Then a smile. "I was looking for you. Where did you go?"

Dawson's felt his mood surge, but he played it easy. "I'm here. I'm there."

"I was hoping we could dance."

"What about Cliff?" Dawson reminded her.

"If you'd rather dance with him . . ." Jen teased.

"You know what I mean."

Jen sighed and continued walking down the hall. "It's a song. A three-minute distraction from life."

Jen really didn't seem to see that there was anything wrong with this picture, did she? Dawson walked beside her. "But he might not like it. You being his date and all." He spit out the word "date" like a rotten fruit.

Jen paused in front of the door to the rest room. "Forget I asked, Dawson," she said, shaking her head.

"But . . ." But what? Jen had asked him to dance. All he'd had to do was say yes. She pushed open the door to the bathroom and went in.

Loser, man. You're a capital *L*, Dawson told himself. He followed her through the door.

Screams bounced off all the tiles and metal and hard, shiny surfaces. A trio of girls lined up at the mirrors over the sinks were all looking at Dawson and shrieking as if Freddy Krueger had just entered the girls' bathroom.

Dawson beat a hasty retreat. What did he think he was doing? Way to go, Leery, he congratulated himself.

"This is embarrassing," Joey said. She and Dawson were sitting at a table. Sitting with the rejects, the wallflowers, the assorted misfits. Watching Jen and Cliff mingle. A bunch of them down there, talking, laughing, kings and queens of the sock hop. Hard to believe she and Dawson had lived in Capeside forever and Jen was only working on week one. "Let's blow this Popsicle stand."

"No. I'm enjoying my misery," Dawson said self-pityingly.

"The ship has sailed, Dawson. And while you sit here on the dock pontificating, the USS *Jennie* is sailing farther and farther out to sea. Haven't you had enough?" Joey asked.

"No, I'm still breathing."

"You hardly know this girl, Dawson."

"That's the magic of it, Joey. True, Jen stepped into my life not more than two seconds ago, but already I feel that connection. That bond that says we're meant to be together. And you can call it wish fulfillment or delusion of the highest adolescent order, but something primal exists between us."

It was just the kind of dramatic speech Dawson liked to deliver. But beneath it, Joey couldn't miss the real hurt in his voice. Or the real yearning. It wasn't something she was used to hearing. "Dawson, you're scaring me. You're doing this Frankenstein-slash-Hyde thing. One minute you're Dawson, and the next you're his psycho alter ego. You've become the sea creature from your own movie."

"So be it," Dawson said. "I can't explain it any more clearly, Joe. The girl is a mystery, but I feel as if I've known her my whole life. It's like the way I feel about you."

Oh? Joey felt her breath catch.

"She challenges me the way you do. She could be you. Only she's Jen."

Joey was on her feet in a flash. What was *that* supposed to be about? She could be you. Only what? She's better than you? Cuter than you? Bigger bra size, for sure. "Well, just let me remind you how your little allegorical horror movie–slash–love story ends. The creature doesn't get the girl. It dies a violent, bloody, horrible death. Rest in peace,

Dawson. It was nice knowing you." Joey pushed her chair back.

"Where are you going?" Dawson asked mildly.

"I'm dead already. Remember?" Joey said. She stormed across the gym floor.

She didn't get far enough fast enough. Suddenly Pacey was grabbing her arm. "Dance with me, Joey," he commanded.

"What!" Had everyone in here gone crazy? Had someone slipped something into the tropical-fish punch?

"Please, you gotta," Pacey said. "I'm trying to make this girl jealous. Please, Joey, put aside all your disgust for one moment in time and dance with me. I beg you."

Joey's mouth tugged down in repulsion. Dawson might have turned into his own sea creature, but Pacey was, after all, the original monster from the deep. And typecast. "I'd rather slide down a razor blade into a huge Jacuzzi full of lemon juice."

But Pacey got his arms around her and started pushing her onto the dance floor.

Joey tried the elbow maneuver that she'd used on Pacey in the film. But this wasn't playacting. The guy was determined. He held her tight and started moving to the slow music. "I'm gonna kill you," Joey said through gritted teeth.

Pacey didn't ease up. "Please. I have cash."

"Let me go before I whip your ass all over this court," Joey threatened.

But Pacey was looking off to the side of the gym.

Joey saw a small, satisfied smile appear on his face. He looked back down at her. "Kiss me," he said.

"You've lost it." Joey yanked away from him. Hard.

Pacey pulled her back in just before she'd fully broken away. "You can hate me forever, Joey, but right now just close your eyes and think of some-one else."

She didn't know what hit her. Pacey grabbed her face in his hands, and his mouth was on her mouth. She felt his lips moving over hers with surprising skill. Her eyes closed. Pacey vanished, and it was someone else. His lips. Just think about his lips— nothing else. She felt herself give in, her mouth melt open, their tongues meet. . . .

And then he was pulling away, and her eyes flew open and—Pacey! The horror of it crashed over her. She brought her hand up and slapped him across the face. Violently, her palm striking his cheek with a loud clap.

"You stagnant sewer filth!" she snarled.

"Time to rewrite," Dawson said to himself. He headed onto the dance floor, where Cliff and Jen were slow dancing in each other's arms. Taking a deep, courageous breath, he tapped Cliff on one massive, muscular shoulder.

"Excuse me. I'd like to cut in."

Cliff and Jen both looked up, startled. "What are you doing, Dawson?" Jen asked.

"Actually, I don't want to cut in. I'd like to take over. I'd like to thank you, Cliff, for showing Jen such a great time for the earlier part of the evening, but I'm here now, of sound mind and body, and can take it from here."

"What are you talking about?" Cliff asked.

Dawson looked at Jen expectantly.

"Yeah, what are you talking about?" Jen echoed.

Dawson was rattled. It wasn't the response he'd anticipated. But he'd let her slip away twice tonight already. Three times and you're out. Even if you're not into baseball, dude.

"I'm talking about you and me," he told Jen earnestly. He turned to Cliff. "Me and her. You see, it's all a little confusing, but all you really need to know, Cliff, is that Jen and I have something going on, and it's still a little raw and undefined, and this is my attempt to clarify the situation." Cliff and Jen had stopped dancing. "So I ask you to do the manly thing and step aside so that I may have a moment with the object of my desire."

Cliff took a step away from Jen and shot her a quizzical look. "Who is this guy?"

Jen looked at Dawson. He looked at her. She didn't look happy. "Dawson, what are you doing?" she asked in a low voice.

"Hey, you're going to have to leave now," Cliff said. "This is too weird."

Around them, people were beginning to stare. Well, it had to be uphill from here, didn't it? "No, you're going to have to leave," Dawson said with a show of bravado. "I'm staying."

Cliff turned to Jen. "What's going on, Jen? Do you want to be with this guy?"

Jen's round, pretty face was drawn. She looked from Dawson to Cliff and back to Dawson.

"Why don't you just leave?" Cliff said threateningly.

"No." Dawson stood his ground. "Why don't you?"

Cliff positioned himself between Dawson and Jen. "And if I don't?" He was looking down at Dawson. He was big. He could win football games with his arm broken in three places.

"Actually, I didn't think it through that far," Dawson said prudently.

But Jen was putting some distance between herself and both of them. "Tell you what," she said, disgust and anger ringing in her voice. "I'll make it easy for both of you. *I'll* go."

And she went.

Dawson and Cliff stood dumbly in the crowd of gently swaying couples. Good rewrite, dude, Dawson told himself. You just lost the girl.

*Chapter 18*

This could easily be the single most horrific night of my life," Dawson said.

Joey stayed safely on one side of him, far away from Pacey. If that sea creature came anywhere near her again, she was going to think about taking out a restraining order. Of course, with Pacey's father and brother making up fully one quarter of the year-round Capeside police force, it might be hard to get it enforced. But Dawson was oblivious to any extra tension between his best buds. Who, after all, could have any dramas that compared to his? The three of them walked home along the harbor as most of the restaurants were closing up for the night.

"I'm a simp," Dawson continued. "Joey, how could you let me do that?"

The moon slid behind a cloud and then out again.

"See? I knew this would turn against me somehow. It would all be my fault."

"And Pacey. My nonexistent friend," Dawson scolded him.

"Sorry man, I was otherwise engaged," Pacey said. He flashed Joey a lewd, secret little grin.

Joey refused to acknowledge him. "At least I didn't desert you," she told Dawson. "I came back."

Dawson whirled on Pacey. "And who is this mystery woman you keep alluding to?"

Pacey sighed. "Unfortunately, the mystery woman remains a mystery even to me," he said.

Dawson didn't pursue it. Not with *Helmets of Glory II* in the making. "I'll bet Jen's lips are pressing against Cliff's at this very moment."

"Don't go there," Joey advised.

They reached the road where Pacey turned off. "Okay, my friends, this is my stop. I'll see you mañana."

"Bye," Dawson said distractedly.

Joey let out a little breath of relief as Pacey detoured. Weird night. She and Dawson walked quietly for a few moments.

"Okay, Joe, let's assess," Dawson finally said. "What have we learned from tonight's 90210 evening?"

That was easy. "We should always stay home on Saturday night and watch movies, because the rewind on the remote of life does not work," Joey answered.

Dawson let out a long breath. "That will not be

a problem now that I've ruined it with Jen. It is officially over."

"It never began, Dawson," Joey corrected him.

Dawson was too dejected to bother with a snappy comeback. "I do feel like the monster from my movie," he said. "There's something going on inside of me I can't control. It's like I have no balance. Everything is a high or a low. It's either hot or cold. Black or white. There's no middle ground anymore. I mean, nothing is just okay."

"I'm too tired to philosophize, Dawson." And she was. They had covered an awful lot of ground in one week.

Dawson studied her and nodded slowly. Joey could see that she'd gotten through. "Do me a favor, when I start to get like this again, " he said, "and I'm sure I will—until this whole adolescent growth process is over—will you simply chain me to my bed and wait for my moment of clarity to come?"

"Can I use leather straps?"

"Not until you explain the Crisco," Dawson said, giving her a shove.

Joey laughed. A real, uncomplicated laugh. "Dawson, you are such a sphincter. You really are. I don't understand how someone can be so self-aware and yet utterly clueless. It escapes me."

"It's my charm," Dawson said.

Joey smiled to herself. Yeah. He was right about that. It *was* his charm. Suddenly she saw a shadow cross Dawson's face.

"Oh, no," he moaned, staring at something in the distance.

# DAWSON'S CREEK

Joey followed his gaze. Not something. Someone.
As in Miss Someone Else. Standing on the pier at
the edge of the harbor, gazing out at the water. She
looked beautiful in the shifting moonlight. Even
Joey saw that.

"What do I do?" Dawson asked. He sounded
genuinely afraid.

"It's your call." Joey couldn't have helped him out
on this one even if she'd wanted to.

"I've pretty much ruined the evening. I may as
well complete it."

"Until no one is left standing," Joey said with
resignation.

"Can I bag on you, Joey?"

"Yeah, you can bag."

Dawson sucked in a breath of sea air. "Wish me
luck."

Joey looked at him, then out at Jen, then back at
Dawson. She ached. But she knew Dawson hurt,
too, and that made her ache even more. "Good
luck, Dawson. I hope you get your kiss."

And in some weird way she meant it. With all
her heart.


"This cannot be happening." Pacey had been here
before. Tamara in the very same spot, looking
moody but beautiful in the soft, twinkling lights of
the harbor. Pacey walking toward her. Just like
last time.

"Miss Jacobs."

She turned. But this time she looked as if she had
been expecting him. "Hi, Pacey."

134

"I feel a strange familiarity creeping over me."

"I thought I might find you here." So she *had* been waiting.

Pacey was instantly flattered. And instantly wary. "Are you here to reiterate what didn't happen—again?" he asked, keeping his distance.

"I thought talking to you might be appropriate."

"Give us a chance to do it all again."

"Only change the ending," Tamara said. "I'm sorry about my behavior, Pacey. I didn't mean to dismiss you, but this whole ordeal has completely thrown me."

Ordeal. Thanks a lot, Miss Jacobs.

"When I saw you at school," she said, "I didn't know what to say. This is without question the most absurd thing I've ever done in my life. Not to mention punishable in a court of law."

"It was just a kiss." Okay, it was some kiss. Still . . .

"No, it was more than that," Tamara said.

Pacey's pulse took off like a speedboat. What was Tamara trying to say?

"It was dead wrong of me, and I can stand here and explain to you my hopelessly troubled state of mind, because you do deserve an explanation for my behavior. But instead of feeding you ten years' worth of therapy, I thought maybe I could get away with a simple apology. Pacey, I'm sorry."

Oh. Sorry, as in sorry it ever happened. The speedboat sputtered to a halt.

"And I hope this hasn't left you with any permanent scars. What I did was wrong . . . and I'm sorry."

Scars? From a kiss? Maybe Tamara wanted to erase the moment, but Pacey didn't. If nothing else, he had the memory of it. The moment when it wasn't about how many years there were between them or which side of the teacher's desk they sat on. The moment when all that existed was the feel of her lips, her body, the desire pulling them together.

"Where do you get off taking all the responsibility for this?" he asked. "I may just be fifteen, but I'm long past the age of accountability." He stopped, realizing how pompous that sounded. "Okay, maybe not within the confines of the judicial system." He gave a short laugh. "But for me. I kissed back. My lips kissed you back."

"Fair enough," Tamara conceded.

"And I don't regret that at all. And you shouldn't, either."

Tamara gave a funny, bittersweet smile. "But it can't happen again, Pacey. From this moment on, our relationship is strictly that of teacher and student. I want that clear."

Too late for that, Pacey thought. "And if I were to object?" He took a step toward her.

"The subject is not up for discussion. You know it has to be this way. For all of the obvious and not so obvious reasons."

Pacey knew she was right. Knew it in his head. Knew it with every logical, rational part of him. But every other part of him knew she was dead wrong.

They stood together, locked in each other's gaze, holding each other without touching. The fire between them burned as white-hot as the scattering of stars overhead.

"This is so unfair," Pacey said softly. "I'm not good with girls, and now I finally meet someone and . . ." His words trailed off. Nothing he could say was going to change the situation.

Tamara reached a tentative hand out to him, then seemed to think better of it and pulled her hand back. "Don't worry, Pacey. That will change. Trust me." Her voice was brimming with tender feelings. Too tender. Pacey could feel himself breaking.

"Yeah, well . . ."

"Good night, Pacey."

"Good night, Tamara."

Pacey tore himself away. Turned and started walking. He could feel her behind him, feel her just standing there. No! It shouldn't be like this! Pacey spun around, closed the gap between them in a few strides, and took her in his arms.

They came together in a fiery kiss. The moment stretched out, potent and intense, obliterating everything else around them. They kissed again. And again.

# Chapter 19

Dawson studied Jen from a few yards away. She was gazing out over the harbor at a small yacht docked nearby. But Dawson doubted she really saw it. On deck a couple drew close together. Jen pulled her light sweater around herself. Drawing into herself. Maybe she *was* watching the couple. Or maybe it was the cool fall air that you could feel riding in on the end of summer.

Dawson fought a silent tug-of-war. Leave bad enough alone? Or keep trying and risk making things worse? Though he wasn't sure that was possible.

"I'm starting to feel like your TV set," Jen said, without shifting her gaze.

Exposed. She'd known he was there all along. "I didn't know what to say," Dawson managed.

"A first?" Jen said flatly. She turned her face toward him.

Dawson stood motionless. Wordless. A first, a second . . . He didn't know what he could say to take back what he'd done.

"I am really angry, Dawson."

"I know." He felt her anger radiating from her like a force field, protecting her, holding him away.

She looked back at the water. "What do you want from me, Dawson?"

"I want to know what's going on between us." No script. Nothing clever. This was real.

"And does that question have to be answered tonight?"

"I'm sorry about tonight, Jen. I got a little scared. Scared I was becoming the 'friend.' "

Jen faced him full on. "Oh. The friend. How awful." There was a bitterness in her voice that he'd never heard before.

"It *is* awful," Dawson said. "I feel as if I'm becoming that friend who lives next door, the one you come and tell all your boy adventures to. And I don't want that to be the case, Jen. I want to be your boy adventure."

"Can't you be both?"

Dawson thought about it. In a strange, backward way, he'd had this conversation before. The first night Joey hadn't slept over. "No," he answered. "Not at fifteen you can't. It's too complicated."

"I see." Jen didn't try to hide her disappointment. Dawson felt his mood dive even lower. Her next words caught him by surprise. "So . . . I'm interested."

"In what?"

She laughed softly. "An adventure. What do I have to do?"

Dawson just stared at her. The smile in her deep-set eyes, the lure of her full mouth, something vaguely mysterious in the way she held herself—she'd never looked quite as beautiful as she did right this second.

"You could kiss me," Dawson dared.

Jen lowered her gaze. Dawson could see the breath go out of her. Feel it go out of him. "You know, I really am a cliché, Dawson. In New York, I was moving really, really fast. So fast, in fact, that I kept stumbling and falling."

Dawson heard the anguish behind her words. For the first time since she'd stepped out of that taxi, he paused to wonder where she'd come from. What place in her mind. If he felt as if he'd known her forever, he suddenly felt he also didn't know her at all. But Jen didn't leave space for questions.

"Here I feel like I'm walking at a steady pace for the first time in a long time," she went on. "And I'm scared that if I kiss you, my knees may buckle and I may stumble, and I don't think I could deal with that right now."

Dawson nodded. Scared of what their kiss could bring? That part he understood just fine. Out on the boat the music changed to Jann Arden singing "You Don't Know Me." The couple on deck moved to the music. Fluidly, intimately.

"Would you like to dance?" Jen asked.

"What? Here?" Dawson looked around as if they were about to get caught out in public with their pajamas on. By whom? And so what? A few cars went by on Bayview Drive. A handful of people, alone or in couples, were strolling on the docks and the beach that curved along the harbor.

"I've been wanting to dance with you all night, Dawson."

Here it was. Another chance. The fresh chance he'd come looking for. Dawson and Jen didn't need any more words. They came together slowly, rhythmically, the music and their feelings taking hold of both of them in unison.

Time slipped away like sand through the cracks in the boardwalk under their feet. There was only now. Only here. Only the cool light of the moon gliding in and out of the clouds, a few stars in the unveiled patches of sky. Jen's perfume mingled with the fresh scent of autumn's arrival. Their breathing—Jen's and Dawson's together—rose and fell like the water lapping at the shore.

They looked into each other's eyes as they danced. "You see, Dawson, the kiss is the end result," Jen whispered. "It's not really important. It's all about desire, and wanting . . ."

"And romance," Dawson whispered.

"Yes." He could feel Jen's breath on his cheek. "Romance . . ."

Well, it wasn't the USS *Jennie* sailing off, after all, Joey thought. It was the USS *Joey*. She climbed into her rowboat and just sat for a while, looking up at Dawson's darkened window.

It seemed like days ago that she'd rowed over for their triple feature. In a different life. Although maybe it had been a different life for longer than she or Dawson really wanted to admit.

It was strange being here without him. Being here and being alone. But the strangest thing was that the ache was gone. For now, at least. She just felt . . . accepting? Empty? Both? She felt as if her little boat had found the calm at the eye of the storm. She'd been swept up by these raging winds, raging feelings, and found a funny little stretch of tranquillity.

Of course, sooner or later she was bound to come crashing down hard. But for now there was only this moment.

Lazily, Joey untied the boat from the dock. It was easy to forget what a pretty place they lived in. Easy not to see what you saw every day. But when you really looked, really stopped to feel it, the world out there could be breathtaking. Awesome enough to dwarf all their little day-to-day problems. Big enough to make the dramas of a handful of people seem pretty insignificant. What was that line from *Casablanca*? "A few people's problems don't add up to a hill of beans in this world." Joey smiled and began rowing.

Close by, a car door slammed. She looked over to see someone parked under a tree by the creek bank, partially hidden. She dipped her oars silently a few times and glided forward for a clearer view.

Mrs. Leery was getting out of the car, coming around to the driver's side. She leaned down to the open window. Kissed the driver good night. It was a deep, long, passionate kiss. Wasn't Mr. Leery getting out too?

It hit Joey all at once. That wasn't Dawson's parents' car. His mother had said she'd be out until midnight. Without his father. As Mrs. Leery straightened up and took a step toward the house, Joey got a good look at the driver's face. Mrs. Leery's co-anchor's face.

Joey felt as if she'd been punched in the gut. Back to you, Bob. So it was true. This wasn't one of Dawson's made-up film fantasy conflicts. Not some carefully crafted drama to play counterpoint to Dawson's perfect life. Except that Dawson's life wasn't so perfect. Joey sat thunderstruck. Frozen with the knowledge.

And the knowledge that Dawson still didn't know.

**Meet the Stars
of the hit
television show produced by
Columbia TriStar Television**

**DAWSON'S CREEK™**

# DAWSON

---

*James Van Der Beek*

Much like the experience of the character he portrays, James Van Der Beek's dedication and talent surfaced at an early age. A mild concussion sidelined his school football career and instead Van Der Beek found himself playing the lead role in a local children's theater production of *Grease*. He fell in love with the theater and continued to perform locally.

"Dawson reminds me of myself when I was 15," say Van Der Beek. "I grew up in a small New England town and vacationed on Cape Cod, where the show takes place, and we both come from loving, supportive homes. We also look alike," jokes the 20-year-old actor.

"Dawson and I were both very impassioned at an early age," explains Van Der Beek. "Dawson is a burgeoning filmmaker, whose overactive imagination and idealism sometimes make him oblivious. He's prone to rejecting reality for a more romantic scenario. He's a bit of an innocent and is frequently off in his own little world, all of which I can definitely relate to."

When Van Der Beek was 16, his mother, noting his intense interest in performing, offered to support his aspirations by accompanying him on daily six-hour round trips into New York City, to test the waters. In spite of landing an agent and manager on their first trip into the city, Van Der Beek spent a year auditioning for commercials without much success.

At 17, Van Der Beek was cast in the off-Broadway play written and directed by Edward Albee, *Finding the Sun.* Juggling the long commute for rehearsals and performances during the play's limited three-month run while attending high school, Van Der Beek credits the play as the defining experience for him as an actor and still managed to finish the school year second in his class.

After his off-Broadway debut, he went on to star in *Shenandoah* at the Goodspeed Opera House. His first screen performance occurred in the 1995 feature film *Angus* as an arrogant jock. Van Der Beek also appeared in the Miramax film *I Love You . . . I Love You Not* with Claire Danes, and most recently in the independent feature film *Harvest.*

An excellent student, Van Der Beek received an academic scholarship to attend Drew University in Madison, New Jersey, where he majored in English and sociology and made the dean's list. He is currently on a leave of absence while shooting DAWSON'S CREEK in Wilmington, North Carolina.

# JOEY

---

Katie Holmes

*E*ighteen-year-old Katie Holmes possesses an exceptional maturity much like Joey Potter, the character she portrays on DAWSON'S CREEK.

Born and raised in Toledo, Ohio, Holmes began acting in high school theater productions in spite of a personal belief that acting careers couldn't be sustained living in the Midwest. "Toledo is a bit bigger than Capeside (the fictional location of DAWSON'S CREEK), but there are similarities," she says. "I'm a small-town girl just like Joey. I wasn't the one that had the boys in high school. I was a little bit of a tomboy and also the youngest in my family, so I thought I knew everything. Like Joey, I made a lot of mistakes, but fortunately I haven't had the tragedy that she's experienced in her life."

Her character, Joey Potter, is something of a tomboy. As Holmes explains, "Joey is a 15-year-old girl that uses a tough attitude as a guard because she's been through so much. She's been hurt so many times that she doesn't want to be vulnerable and put herself out there for everyone. She has to be tough. She lost her mom [to cancer] and her dad's in prison. She lives with her unwed and pregnant sister and her sister's boyfriend. Her relationship with Dawson has been the only stable thing in her life and now it's beginning to change."

The stability and importance of friends played a

significant role in Holmes's life as well when she chose to honor her commitment to friends and classmates by performing in the school production of *Damn Yankees* instead of going to Los Angeles on a callback from the producers and casting agents for DAWSON'S CREEK. Fortunately, the producers were able to reschedule the audition and Holmes won the role of Joey Potter.

A captivating newcomer to the entertainment world, Holmes has experienced incredible success, landing major roles in both feature films and television projects while participating in only a handful of auditions. Her very first professional audition resulted in a plum role in the award-winning film *The Ice Storm*, directed by Ang Lee (*Sense and Sensibility*). The film, which recently won the screenplay award from the Cannes Film Festival, stars Kevin Kline, Sigourney Weaver, Elijah Wood, and Joan Allen and depicts the sexual revolution of the 1970s.

Having graduated from high school, Holmes is now living in Wilmington, North Carolina, while working on DAWSON'S CREEK.

# PACEY

───

*Joshua Jackson*

*B*orn in Vancouver, 19-year-old Joshua Jackson
spent his formative years in California, moving with
his family back to Vancouver at the age of eight. It
was there that he launched his professional career,
appearing in a series of television commercials pro-
moting tourism in British Columbia. While his family shuttled between Vancouver and California,
Jackson also sang with the San Francisco Boys'
Chorus.

In describing his character, Pacey, Jackson ad-
mits, "Four years ago, I had similar issues to what
Pacey is dealing with. We both grew up in a
community-based atmosphere. He grew up in a
much smaller town, which has its own limitations
and benefits, but I grew up in a community where
I knew everybody in the neighborhood, went to
school with all the same kids and spent a decade of
my life with the same people. Like Pacey, I also
have an offbeat sense of humor and I enjoy laughing, having a good time, and often get myself in
trouble for it. But neither of us is mischievous for
mischief's sake. Pacey's in his own world, doing his
own thing, which unfortunately seems to offend a
lot of people."

Jackson continues, "Pacey's basically an outsider
at school who also feels disconnected from his family. He's always been told he's a screwup and isn't
going to succeed, so he feels he can do anything he

likes and has nothing to lose. He finds a group of friends that take him for what he is and both understand and appreciate his oddball quality. Pacey's also the odd man out in his family. His father is the sheriff of Capeside and his brother is a deputy. He is closer to his mother and sisters, but his sisters are off at school. Because of this family dynamic, Pacey is much more comfortable with women. I was raised among females; it was just me, my mom, and my sister, and I'm more comfortable being around women because of that too."

Unlike his DAWSON'S CREEK character, however, Jackson excelled at an early age. Landing his first feature-film role in Michael Bortman's *Crooked Hearts* for MGM/Pathe, Jackson's stage debut followed in 1991, when he played the lead role of Charlie in the Seattle production of *Willy Wonka and the Chocolate Factory*. Since then, Jackson has appeared in such films as *Andre the Seal*, *Tombstone*, *Digger*, and *Magic in the Water*, as well as all three of Disney's *The Mighty Ducks* features, portraying the coach's prodigy and the team's voice of reason, Charlie. Jackson has also recently completed principal photography for Bryan Singer's latest film, *Apt Pupil*, starring Ian McKellen and produced by Mike Medavoy.

His recent television projects include two Showtime Contemporary Classics, *Robin of Locksley*, based on the Robin Hood legend, and *Ronnie and Julie*, an updated version of Shakespeare's *Romeo and Juliet*. Jackson has also appeared in *Champs*, the DreamWorks/ABC series created and produced by *Family Ties* producer Gary David Goldberg.

As a regular on DAWSON'S CREEK, Jackson now lives in Wilmington, North Carolina, during production.

# JEN

---

*Michelle Williams*

Michelle Williams, like her character Jennifer Lindley on DAWSON'S CREEK, is making the transition from big city to small-town life. The 17-year-old actress moved from Los Angeles to Wilmington, North Carolina, the production location for the series. As Williams recounts, "It's quite a change from Los Angeles. It's beautiful and a nice pace for a while, but at first it was a strange switch from the city and traffic. Having the experience of moving from a big city to a small town does make it easier to relate to Jen, however."

Williams explains that her character "is an outsider coming to Capeside from a fast-paced New York lifestyle. Ostensibly she's come to help her strict grandmother care for her seriously ailing grandfather, but she's hiding a troubled past. More sophisticated and worldly than the other three teen characters, she's an old soul, having done a lot and grown up fast. I think a part of Jen is really looking to regain her innocence and lead the quintessential teenage life, and she wants to fit in with these more carefree kids. But there's another part of her that still longs for the city lights, taxi rides, bars, and clubs. She made some mistakes, and got sent to Capeside by her parents in hopes that she'd begin to realize she should slow down and change her ways."

While Williams may be a bit homesick for big city

life herself, she is no stranger to the country, having grown up in an idyllic spot in Montana. After her family moved to San Diego, she took advantage of the proximity of Hollywood to explore an acting career, which quickly took off. At 16, after obtaining an accelerated high school degree, she moved to Los Angeles full time to pursue her craft. Most recently, she portrayed Michelle Pfeiffer's daughter in Propaganda Films' *A Thousand Acres*, starring Jessica Lange, Michelle Pfeiffer, and Jason Robards. Williams has also appeared in numerous theater productions. On television, she has won guest appearances on series including *Step by Step* and *Home Improvement*, as well as roles in the television movies *A Mother's Justice* and *Killing Mr. Griffin*. Her additional feature film credits include *Species*, *Lassie*, and *Time Master*.

While living in Wilmington to shoot DAWSON'S CREEK, Williams enjoys reading as many books as she can in her spare time.

"Meet the Stars" material provided courtesy of Columbia TriStar Interactive.

## About the Author

Jennifer Baker is the author of over thirty novels for young readers and a creator of Web-based entertainment and dramas. She lives in New York City with her husband and son.

Don't miss any of these
*Dawson's Creek*™ books!
Read more about
*Joey, Dawson, Pacey,* and *Jen*
in four new, original
*Dawson's Creek*™ stories.

Long Hot Summer
Major Meltdown
Shifting Into Overdrive
Double Exposure

Coming soon from Channel 4 Books.
Check your bookstore to see
if they're in yet.